PENGUIN REFERENCE

Penguin Pocket Jokes

David Pickering graduated in English from St Peter's College, Oxford. An experienced reference books compiler, he has contributed to (and often been sole author and editor of) some 200 reference books, mostly in the areas of the arts, language, local history and popular interest. These include a *Dictionary of Theatre* (1988), an *Encyclopedia of Pantomime* (1993), *Brewer's Twentieth-Century Music* (1994; 1997), a *Dictionary of Superstitions* (1995), a *Dictionary of Witchcraft* (1996), *The Penguin Dictionary of First Names* (1999; 2004) and the *Pears Factfinder* (2002). He lives in Buckingham with his wife and two sons.

PENGUIN POCKET
JOKES

David Pickering

PENGUIN BOOKS

PENGUIN BOOKS

Published by the Penguin Group
Penguin Books Ltd, 80 Strand, London WC2R 0RL, England
Penguin Group (USA) Inc., 375 Hudson Street, New York, New York 10014, USA
Penguin Group (Canada), 90 Eglinton Avenue East, Suite 700, Toronto, Ontario, Canada M4P 2Y3
(a division of Pearson Penguin Canada Inc.)
Penguin Ireland, 25 St Stephen's Green, Dublin 2, Ireland (a division of Penguin Books Ltd)
Penguin Group (Australia), 250 Camberwell Road, Camberwell, Victoria 3124, Australia
(a division of Pearson Australia Group Pty Ltd)
Penguin Books India Pvt Ltd, 11 Community Centre, Panchsheel Park, New Delhi – 110 017, India
Penguin Group (NZ), cnr Airborne and Rosedale Roads, Albany, Auckland 1310, New Zealand
(a division of Pearson New Zealand Ltd)
Penguin Books (South Africa) (Pty) Ltd, 24 Sturdee Avenue,
Rosebank, Johannesburg 2196, South Africa

Penguin Books Ltd, Registered Offices: 80 Strand, London WC2R 0RL, England

www.penguin.com

First published 2006
4

Copyright © David Pickering, 2006
All rights reserved

The moral right of the author has been asserted

Set in 8.19/10.697 pt PostScript ITC Stone Sans
Typeset by Rowland Phototypesetting Ltd, Bury St Edmunds, Suffolk
Printed in England by Clays Ltd, St Ives plc

ISBN-13: 978–0–14–102748–7

Contents

Introduction

While some people can retain a store of hundreds of jokes in their memory with apparent ease, others complain that they find it difficult to remember a single one. This book is designed to appeal to both types, enriching the supply of seasoned joke-tellers as well as serving as an entertaining aide-memoire to those whose memory needs some prompting.

This collection of jokes includes numerous perennial favourites as well as many less well-known jokes, puns and humorous quotations. At its heart is a core of several hundred classic jokes that will be immediately familiar to most readers, among them elephant jokes, chicken-crossing-roads jokes, cannibal jokes, knock-knock jokes, doctor jokes, waiter jokes, people-in-pubs jokes, school jokes, animal jokes, ghost jokes, skeleton jokes, vampire jokes, mother-in-law jokes and a host of other categories. Also included are timeless riddles and puns, plus a smattering of humorous comical observations by wits ranging from Groucho Marx and Bob Hope to Tommy Cooper and Woody Allen.

The jokes themselves vary from succinct one-liners to longer story-jokes of the type that are commonly employed to enliven speeches. The range of jokes and witticisms included should mean that there is something here to appeal to every sense of humour. And if it's all too much, don't forget what to do if you split your sides laughing – run till you get a stitch.

My thanks go to my two sons, Edward and Charles Pickering, for helping to compile this collection.

David Pickering

A

Aardvarks *See* **Anteaters**.

Abominable snowmen

Has anyone ever captured an abominable snowman?
Not yeti.

What do abominable snowmen drink on top of the
Himalayas?
High tea.

How do abominable snowmen get to the shops?
By icicle.

What's the difference between an abominable snowman
and an intelligent blonde?
There have been actual sightings of abominable snowmen.

See also **Monsters**.

Absence

Why did the biscuit cry?
Because his mother had been a wafer so long.

What did the cowboy say when he found his dog was missing?
'Doggone!'

Police Officer Why aren't you at school today?
Pupil I'm sick.
Police Officer Sick of what?
Pupil Sick of school.

Father I hear you skipped school to play football.
Son No, I didn't, and I have the fish to prove it!

Teacher You! Did you miss school yesterday?
Pupil Yes, but not very much.

'Did you miss me while I was away?'
'Oh, have you been away?'

See also **Punctuality**.

Absentmindedness

'Knock, knock.'
'Who's there?'
'Arfur.'
'Arfur who?'
'Arfur got.'

'I wish you would pay a little attention.'
'I'm paying as little as I can.'

An old man stops a pretty girl in the park. 'I suffer from amnesia. Do I come here often?'

The vicar called in the other day. He said that at my age, I should be thinking more about the 'Hereafter'. I told him that I do, all the time. No matter where I am, in the kitchen, in the bedroom, in the garage, I always ask myself, 'Now, what am I here after?'

A young woman is concerned to find an old man weeping loudly in the street and asks him what the matter is. 'Everything is perfect,' he replies between sobs. 'My pension pays me a fortune, I have a lovely house, a beautiful young wife and my own private jet.' 'So why are you crying?' asks the young woman. 'I can't remember where I live!'

'Doctor, doctor, I've got amnesia!'
'Go home and forget about it.'

'Doctor, doctor, I keep forgetting things!'
'How long have you had this problem?'
'What problem?'

See also **Age**.

Accidents

Did you hear about the butcher's boy who sat on the bacon slicer?
He got a little behind in his deliveries.

Did you hear about the woman who fell into the upholstery machine?
She's fully recovered.

Did you hear about the man who fell into the
lens-grinding machine?
He made a real spectacle of himself.

Did you hear about the Indian cook who dropped a pot of
curry on his head?
It put him in a korma.

Did you hear about the secretary who lost the tips of two
fingers in an accident with her typewriter?
Now she does shorthand.

There once was a man name of Crocket
Who stuck his foot in a socket.
Then along came a witch
Who turned on the switch
And Crocket went up like a rocket.

There was an old man from Carlisle
Who sat down one day on a stile.
The paint it was wet,
So he's sitting there yet;
But he hopes to get off with a file.

There was a young man from Quebec
Who wrapped both his legs round his neck,
But then he forgot
How to undo the knot,
And now he's an absolute wreck.

Why was the sword-swallower put in prison?
He coughed and killed two people.

What happened when Mum dropped a roast turkey?
The downfall of Turkey, the break-up of China and the
overthrow of Greece.

A parachutist jumps from a plane only to find his
parachute won't open. As he plummets towards the
ground, still trying to open his chute, he passes another
man going up. 'Know anything about parachutes?' the
parachutist shouts. 'No,' says the other man, 'know
anything about gas cookers?'

Why did the aircraft land on top of a house?
Because the landing lights were on.

Did you hear about the campfire that got out of control?
The flames were in tents.

A lorry carrying red paint crashed into a lorry carrying
purple paint. Both drivers were marooned.

Newsflash: A lorry carrying copies of the new *Thesaurus*
crashed today. Witnesses were startled, stunned, amazed,
staggered, taken aback, aghast . . .

Did you hear about the man who was told that most car
accidents happen within two miles of home?
He moved.

Did you hear about the man who lost his left arm and leg
in a car crash?
He's all right now.

A doctor and a lawyer crash into each other in a country
lane. Neither is hurt, but the cars are a mess. Seeing that
the doctor is dazed, the lawyer offers him a drink from his
hip flask. The doctor accepts it gratefully, drinks deeply,

then hands the hip flask back. The lawyer puts it in his pocket. 'Aren't you having one?' the doctor asks. 'I'll have one later,' says the lawyer, 'after the police have gone.'

'Doctor, doctor, I've broken my arm in two places!' 'Well, don't go back there again, then.'

Accountants

When does a person decide to become an accountant? When he realizes he doesn't have the charisma to be an undertaker.

A woman was told she had only six months to live. 'What shall I do?' she cried. 'Marry an accountant,' said the doctor. 'Will that make me live longer?' she asked. 'No,' said the doctor, 'but it will seem longer.'

If an accountant's wife can't get to sleep, what does she say? 'Tell me about work today, dear.'

A young accountant has been accused of sharp practice. The senior partner turns to him and asks, 'You do know what Ethics is, don't you?' The young accountant is offended. 'Of course I know what Ethics is. It's a county in southern England.'

What did the terrorist who hijacked a plane full of accountants threaten to do if his demands weren't met? Release one every hour.

What is the difference between a tragedy and a catastrophe?

A tragedy is a shipful of accountants being sunk in a storm. A catastrophe is when they can all swim.

Old accountants never die, they just lose their balances.

See also **Business**; **Money**; **Taxation**.

Acting

'The secret of acting is sincerity. If you can fake that, you've got it made.' *(George Burns)*

Did you hear about the actor who fell through the floor? It was just a stage he was going through.

How do you kill a bad variety act?
Go for the juggler.

What do ghosts enjoy at the theatre?
Phantomimes.

Old actors never die, they just drop apart.

Adultery

Moses went up the mountain to negotiate the Commandments with God. His people anxiously awaited his return. Eventually, an exhausted Moses came back down the slope. 'Well,' he announced, 'there's good news and bad news. The good news is that I got Him down to ten. The bad news is that adultery's still in.'

A man arrives home and finds his wife kissing his best friend. At this he rushes to his garage, grabs his gun and holds it to his head. 'I can't bear this! My wife and my best friend kissing each other! I'm going to shoot myself!' His wife stares at him and then starts to laugh. 'I don't know why you're laughing,' retorts the outraged husband, 'you're next!'

A managing director is concerned to find one of his employees is suffering badly from stress. One afternoon he takes the man aside and gives him some advice: 'Whenever I feel stressed I take two weeks off and stay at home to be pampered by my wife. It always does the trick. You should try it!' The man thanks him for his advice and takes two weeks off. Two weeks later he returns to work, rejuvenated and full of energy. 'I see you followed my advice,' observes the managing director. 'I certainly did,' replies the employee. 'It was wonderful! And I had no idea you had such a nice house!'

'Eighty per cent of married men cheat in America. The rest cheat in Europe.' *(Jackie Mason)*

'There is one thing I would break up over, and that is if she caught me with another woman. I won't stand for that.' *(Steve Martin)*

See also **Divorce**; **Husbands and wives**; **Marriage**; **Sex**.

Aeroplanes See **Aviation**.

Age

What did the big candle say to the little candle?
'You're too young to go out.'

What did the big tap call the little tap?
A little squirt.

What did the little tap call the big tap?
A big drip.

'Knock, knock.'
'Who's there?'
'A little old lady.'
'A little old lady who?'
'I didn't know you could yodel!'

Why did the sword-swallower stop when he had
swallowed only half a sword?
He was having a mid-knife crisis.

What's the best way to get a youthful figure?
Ask a woman her age.

'How old is your wife?'
'Approaching thirty.'
'From which direction?'

'Have you lived here all your life?'
'Not yet.'

'I've found the secret of eternal youth. I lie about my age.'
(Bob Hope)

'Three things happen when you get to my age. First your
memory starts to go, and I've forgotten the other two.'
(attributed to British politician Denis Healey)

'By the time you're eighty years old you've learned
everything. You only have to remember it.' *(George Burns)*

See also **Absentmindedness**.

Alcohol

Our Lager,
Which art in barrels,
Hallowed be thy drink.
Thy will be drunk,
I will be drunk,
At home as in the tavern.
Give us this day our foamy head,
And forgive us our spillages,
As we forgive those who spill against us.
And lead us not into incarceration,
But deliver us from hangovers.
For thine is the Beer, the Bitter and the Lager,
Barmen.

An old lady who came from Kilbride
Ate so many apples she died.
The apples fermented
Inside the lamented –
Making cider inside 'er inside!

One tequila, two tequila, three tequila, floor.

What do you call an empty beer glass?
A juggernaut.

How many men does it take to open a beer?
None. It should be opened by the time she brings it to him.

What's the difference between a dog and a fox?
About eight beers.

Wine improves with age. The older you get, the more you like it.

Whisky is a wonderful drink. It makes you see double and feel single.

What do you call a rhino who drinks too much?
A whino.

'Why do they call your father-in-law the exorcist?'
'Every time he visits he rids the house of spirits.'

What is a drunkard's last drink?
His bier.

A man is sitting in a pub on his own, staring into his drink. For a joke, another drinker comes up to him and drains the man's glass in one swig. The first man bursts into tears. 'Sorry, mate,' says the second man, embarrassed, 'it was only a joke. Let me buy you another.' The first man dries his eyes. 'You don't understand – this has been the worst day of my life. First I lose my job, then my car is stolen, I lose my wallet on the train, and when I come home I find my wife has left me. Finally, I come to this pub to end it all and then you turn up and drink my poison . . .'

'A woman drove me to drink and I never even had the courtesy to thank her.' *(W. C. Fields)*

'I drink to make other people interesting.' *(Groucho Marx)*

See also **Drink**; **Pubs**.

Aliens

What do you call a fat alien?
An extra-cholesterol.

What did the alien say to the petrol pump?
'Take your fingers out of your ears and listen to me!'

How does an alien count to twenty-seven?
On its fingers.

What do aliens cook their dinner in?
Frying saucers.

What's E.T. short for?
Because he has little legs.

See also **Astronauts**; **Space**.

Alphabet

Why is B the hottest letter of the alphabet?
Because it makes oil boil.

Why is a naughty boy like the letter D?
They both make ma mad.

In English what comes after E?
N.

Why is the letter G scary?
It turns a host into a ghost.

Why shouldn't you put the letter M in the fridge?
Because it changes ice into mice.

Have you ever seen a duchess?
It's exactly the same as an English S.

Why is S the witches' favourite letter?
Because it turns cream into scream.

What letter can you find in a cup?
T.

Why were the letters U, V, W, X, Y and Z late for the tea party?
Because they all come after T.

What three letters turn a girl into a woman?
A G E.

Which three letters are full of power?
N R G.

Which two letters are the most jealous?
N V.

'I bet I can say the alphabet quicker than you.'
'The alphabet – beat you!'

See also **Spelling**.

Anatomy

Why do tall people have long arms?
Because otherwise their arms wouldn't reach their hands.

What has two arms, two wings, two tails, three heads,
three bodies and eight legs?
A man on a horse holding a chicken.

What did the left eye say to the right eye?
'Between you and me, something smells!'

How many ears did Davy Crockett have?
Three: his right ear, his left ear and his wild front ear.

How do very small people communicate with each other?
With microphones.

There once was a girl of New York
Whose body was lighter than cork;
She had to be fed
For six weeks upon lead
Before she went out for a walk.

Did you hear about the fat man on the bus?
When he got up he offered his seat to three women.

My auntie is so fat that when she hung her nightie on the
washing line a troop of boy scouts moved in.

Did you hear about the fat child who tried to run away
from home?
He gave up because the fridge was too heavy.

See also **Diets**; **Food**.

Angling See *Fishing*.

Animals

What did the daddy buffalo say to his son when he left home?
'Bison.'

What's the difference between a buffalo and a bison?
You can't wash your hands in a buffalo.

How do elks disguise themselves?
With false moosetaches.

What do you call two hedgehogs?
A prickly pear.

What do you get if you cross a hyena with gravy?
Laughing stock.

Consider the poor hippopotamus:
His life is unduly monotonous.
He lives half asleep
At the edge of the deep,
And his face is as big as his bottom is.

What do you get if you cross a leopard with a bunch of flowers?
A beauty spot.

What do porcupines like to eat?
Prickled onions.

How do you stop a rhino charging?
Take away its credit card.

How do you tell a weasel from a stoat?
A weasel's weasily recognized, but a stoat's stoatally different.

What do yaks chat to each other about?
The latest gnus.

See also **Anteaters**; **Bears**; **Birds**; **Camels**; **Cats**; **Cows**; **Crabs**; **Crocodiles**; **Deer**; **Dinosaurs**; **Dogs**; **Donkeys**; **Elephants**; **Fish**; **Frogs and toads**; **Giraffes**; **Goats**; **Gorillas**; **Horses**; **Insects**; **Kangaroos**; **Lions**; **Mice**; **Monkeys**; **Noah's ark**; **Octopuses**; **Pets**; **Pigs**; **Polar bears**; **Rabbits**; **Sharks**; **Sheep**; **Shellfish**; **Skunks**; **Slugs and snails**; **Snakes**; **Tigers**; **Tortoises**; **Vets**; **Whales**; **Wolves**; **Worms**; **Zebras**; **Zoos**.

Anteaters

Why aren't ants scared of anteaters?
Because a little aardvark never hurt anyone.

What do you get if you cross an anteater with a dog?
An aardbark.

Where do anteaters go out to eat?
In restaurants.

Why don't anteaters ever get ill?
Because they are full of antibodies.

See also **Ants**.

Ants

What ants are the biggest?
Elephants.

What ants are bigger than elephants?
Giants.

Which ants are the smallest?
Infants.

Why do male ants swim better than female ants?
Because they are buoyant.

What do you get if you cross some ants with some ticks?
All sorts of antics.

What do you call an ant who lives with your great-uncle?
Your great-ant.

What do you call an ant who hates school?
A truant.

What do you call a 100-year-old ant?
An antique.

What do you call a well-dressed ant?
Elegant.

What do you call an ant who lives on his own?
Independant.

What do you call an ant who can't play the piano?
Discordant.

What kind of ant is good at maths?
An accountant.

Where do ants go on holiday?
Frants.

See also **Anteaters**.

Army See **Soldiers**.

Art

Teacher I told the class to draw a cow eating grass, but you
have drawn only a cow.
Pupil The cow ate all the grass.

Teacher I told you to draw a pony and trap, but you have
drawn only a pony.
Pupil I thought the pony would draw the trap.

What do you get if you give crayons to your children?
A gift to make your kin scrawl.

Why did the picture go to jail?
Because it was framed.

What kind of paintings do cats like best?
Pawtraits.

What do you call an American drawing?
A Yankee doodle.

What colours did the artist paint the sun and the wind?
The sun rose and the wind blew.

Why did the artist take a pencil to bed with him?
To draw the curtains.

What did the pencil sharpener say to the pencil?
'Stop going in circles and get to the point!'

What do you get if you cross an artist with a police officer?
A brush with the law.

What is an artery?
The study of paintings.

'What do you think of my latest sculpture? I'd value your opinion.'
'It's worthless.'
'I know, but I'd like to hear it all the same.'

Astronauts

How do you get a baby astronaut to sleep?
You rocket.

What do you do if you see a spaceman?
You park in it, man.

Where do astronauts leave their spaceships?
At parking meteors.

What do astronauts have before going into space?
A big launch.

What is an astronaut's watch called?
A lunatic.

Why couldn't the astronauts land on the moon?
It was full.

If athletes get athlete's foot, what do astronauts get?
Missile-toe.

What is a specimen?
An Italian astronaut.

Old astronauts never die, they just go to another world.

See also **Aliens**; **Space**.

Athletics

Who was the fastest runner of all time?
Adam, because he came first in the human race.

Did you hear about the marathon runner who ran for
three hours but only moved two feet?
He only had two feet.

How do you start a jelly race?
'Get set . . .'

How do you start a pudding race?
Say go.

How do fireflies start their races?
'Ready, steady, glow!'

Who won the vampires' race?
They finished neck and neck.

What's the longest punctuation mark?
The 100-metre dash.

See also **Sports**.

Automobiles *See* **Cars**; **Motorists**.

Aviation

If flying is so safe, why do they call airports terminals?

What do you call a flying elephant?
A jumbo jet.

Why do aircraft always fly past Peter Pan's house?
Because of the sign saying 'Never Never Land'.

Why did the child do his homework in an aeroplane?
He was in higher education.

Why did the old lady always fly with a bomb in her suitcase?
Because she had been told that the chances of there being two bombs on the same plane were a billion to one.

An aeroplane is just a few minutes into a transatlantic flight when the captain announces, 'Ladies and gentlemen, one of our engines has failed. There is no cause for alarm. Our flight will take an hour longer than scheduled, but we still have three engines left.' A few minutes later the captain comes on the intercom once more. 'Another engine has failed. The flight will now take an additional two hours, but we can still fly on two engines.' Half an hour later the captain's voice is heard again. 'One more engine has failed and the flight will now take an additional three hours. There is no need to worry – we still have one engine left.' At this one of the passengers turns to the man next to him and mutters in annoyance, 'If we lose one more engine, we'll be up here all day!'

An aeroplane carrying an Englishman, a Frenchman, a Texan and a Mexican gets into difficulty far out over the ocean. The pilot tells the passengers that if three of them jump out then the fourth might just make it. The Englishman swallows hard, shouts, 'God save the Queen!' and jumps out of the aeroplane. Next the Frenchman shouts, 'Vive la France!' and similarly jumps out of the plane. The Texan sighs then gets to his feet, shouts, 'Remember the Alamo!' and throws out the Mexican.

Newsflash: Ireland's worst air crash took place earlier today when a two-seater plane crashed into a cemetery. Irish rescue workers have so far recovered nearly 2,000 bodies.

If an aircraft crashed on the border of England and Scotland, where would the survivors be buried?
Nowhere – they survived.

What's red, flies and wobbles?
A jellycopter.

Did you hear about the blonde whose helicopter crashed?
She was cold so she turned off the fan.

Old pilots never die, they just go to a higher plane.

B

Babies

Why did the pregnant woman eat a rubber?
She wanted a bouncing baby.

Mr Bigger, Mrs Bigger and Baby Bigger were all big, but
which was biggest?
Baby Bigger, because he was just a little bigger.

A young couple came home with their first baby. The wife
suggested that her husband change the baby's nappy. 'Not
now,' he replied, 'next time.' Later that evening the wife
tried again, 'Can you change the baby's nappy?' 'You don't
understand,' said the man patiently, 'I meant the next baby.'

A man met a woman, with a baby in her arms, weeping
bitterly on a park bench. 'What's the matter?' he inquired.
'I'm upset because everyone thinks my baby is ugly.' The
man soothed her and gave a handkerchief to dry her eyes.
'Let me buy you a cup of tea,' the man offered. 'You'll feel
better, then.' 'Thank you,' said the woman, mopping her
eyes. 'And how about a banana for your monkey?'

Baldness

A man with thinning hair was shocked to find that he was
going to be charged £20 for a trim. 'I haven't got much

hair – how come it's so expensive?' 'Well,' explained the barber, 'it's £5 for the cut and £15 for the search fee.'

'Doctor, doctor, my hair keeps falling out! Can you give me something to keep it in?'
'Have this paper bag.'

What do you call a pen with no hair?
A bald point.

Why do bald men have no use for keys?
Because they have lost their locks.

A bald-headed man was much impressed by a sign outside a barber's that read: 'Bald? Try our instant treatment! £100 for a head of hair just like mine!' The man decided to try out the treatment and handed over £100. The barber pocketed the money, then shaved his own hair off.

Newsflash: A lorryload of wigs have been stolen in Manchester. The police are combing the area.

See also **Hair**.

Banks

What do you call a bank manager sitting in a tree?
A branch manager.

What's the difference between a dead bank manager and a dead skunk when they get run over?
There are skid marks by the skunk.

Old bankers never die, they just lose interest.

'A bank is a place that will lend you money if you can prove that you don't need it.' *(Bob Hope)*

See also **Money**.

Bars *See* **Pubs**.

Bears

What do you call a bear with no ear?
A B.

Why are bears large, brown and hairy?
If they were small, round and white they'd be eggs.

Which side of a bear has the most fur?
The outside.

What animal do you look like in the bath?
A little bear.

Why was the little bear so spoiled?
Because its mother panda'd to its every whim.

What did Paddington Bear and Winnie-the-Pooh take on holiday?
The bear essentials.

What do you get if you cross a grizzly bear and a harp?
A bear-faced lyre.

See also **Polar bears**; **Teddy bears**.

Bees

Why do bees hum?
Because they don't know the words.

What is a baby bee?
A little humbug.

What did the bee say to the flower?
'Hello, honey.'

What do bees say in summer?
' 'Swarm.'

Why is there always a shortage of honey in Brighton?
Because there is only one B in Brighton.

What did the sensible bee say to the naughty bee?
'Bee-hive yourself.'

Why did the queen bee kick out all of the other bees?
Because they kept droning on and on.

What do you call a bee who's had a spell put on him?
Bee-witched.

What do bees chew?
Bumble gum.

What did the confused bee say?
'To bee or not to bee?'

Where do librarians keep bees?
In archives.

What do bees do if they want to use public transport?
They wait at a buzz stop.

What did the bee say to the fly?
'I'll give you a buzz later.'

What's more risky than being with a fool?
Fooling with a bee.

Small boy Ow! That bee stung my arm!
Mother Let me put some cream on it.
Small boy Don't be silly. It's miles away by now!

What do you get if you cross a bee with a doorbell?
A humdinger.

What do you get if you cross a bee with a lizard?
A blizzard.

Bigamy

'Bigamy is having one wife too many. Monogamy is the same.' *(Oscar Wilde)*

There was an old man of Lyme
Who married three wives at a time.
When asked, 'Why a third?'
He replied, 'One's absurd,
And bigamy, sir, is a crime.'

Why did the bigamist cross the aisle?
To get to the other bride.

What is the maximum penalty for bigamy?
Two mothers-in-law.

Did you hear about the man who married both Kate and Edith?
He wanted to have his Kate and Edith too.

What is a bigamist?
An Italian fog.

'Bigamy is the only crime on the books where two rites make a wrong.' *(Bob Hope)*

See also **Marriage**.

Birds

What do you call a bird with no eye?
A brd.

Which side of a bird has the most feathers?
The outside.

What is the most common illness among birds?
Flu.

Why do birds fly south in the winter?
Because it's too far to walk.

What do birds use in case of emergency?
Sparrowchutes.

How do robins keep fit?
They do worm-ups.

What do you get if you cross a pigeon with an elephant?
Anxious pedestrians.

What do you call a woodpecker with no beak?
A headbanger.

What is a goose?
An animal that grows down as it grows up.

What is a baby turkey called?
A goblet.

Why do seagulls fly over the sea?
Because if they flew over the bay they would be bagels.

Which bird can write underwater?
A ballpoint penguin.

What bird is always out of breath?
A puffin.

What is the strongest bird?
A crane.

What do you call a rude bird?
A mockingbird.

What bird lives underground?
A mynah bird.

Why are peacocks so unpopular?
They're always spreading tales.

What do you call a canary in a food blender?
Shredded tweet.

Why do storks stand on one leg?
Because they'd fall over if they lifted the other one.

What birds spend all their time on their knees?
Birds of prey.

Two hawks watch a jet hurtle overhead. 'Look at that!'
says the first. 'So what?' says the second. 'I'd go that fast if
my tail was on fire.'

How can you tell that eagles are smarter than chickens?
Have you ever heard of an eagle-burger?

What is the difference between 'unlawful' and 'illegal'?
'Unlawful' means 'against the law', whereas 'illegal' is a
'sick bird'.

Why did the child sprinkle bird seed on the ground?
He hoped to grow some birds.

Why is the sky so high?
So the birds won't bump their heads.

*See also **Chickens**; **Ducks**; **Owls**; **Parrots**.*

Birth See *Babies*.

Birthdays

What do you always get on your birthday?
Another year older.

Why are birthdays good for you?
The more you have, the longer you live.

When is Luke Skywalker's birthday?
May the Fourth (be with you).

'When is your birthday?'
'The third of September.'
'Which year?'
'Every year.'

Did you hear about the candle shop that burned down?
Everyone stood round singing 'Happy Birthday'.

*See also **Age**.*

Blondes *See **Dumb blondes**.*

Book titles

A Clifftop Tragedy by Eileen Dover
A Young Man's Guide to Dating by Caesar Titely
At the North Pole by I. C. Blast
At the South Pole by Ann Tarctic
Better Gardening by Anita Lawn
Bubbles in the Bath by Ivor Windy-Bottom
Bullying is Wrong by Howard U. Lykit
Carpet Laying by Walter Wall
Dating Period Furniture by Anne Teak
Dealing with Alcoholism by Carrie M. Holme
Diary of a Bank Robber by Hans Upp
Eating Garlic by Y. I. Malone
Escape to the New Forest by Lucinda Woods
Gone With the Wind by Rufus Blownoff
How I Won the Grand National by Rhoda Winner
How to be Stupid by M. T. Head
How to Succeed by Vic Tree
Improve Your Memory by Ivor Gott

Influenza by Mike Robe
Into Battle by Sally Forth
Jungle Fever by Amos Quito
Keeping Caged Birds by Ken Airey
Keeping Cheerful by Mona Lott
Lumberjacks by Tim Burr
Magic for Beginners by Beatrix Ster
Moving Day by Ivor Newhouse
My Political Memoirs by Lisa Lott
On the Beach by C. Shaw
Pain and Sorrow by Ann Guish
Primary School by L. M. Entree
Rice Growing by Paddy Field
Road Transport by Laurie Driver
Scalp Disorders by Dan Druff
Show Jumping by Jim Carner
So Tired by Carrie Mee
Strong Winds by Gail Force
Swimming the Channel by Frances Near
The Bad Striker by Misty Goal
The Bank Raid by Dinah Mite
The Burglar by Robin Banks
The Cannibal's Daughter by Henrietta Mann
The Haunted Room by Hugo First
The Insomniac by Eliza Wake
The Library Thieves by M. T. Shelves
The Millionaire by Ivor Fortune
The Runaway Bull by Gay Topen
The Tiger's Revenge by Claude Body
The World of Hairdressing by Aaron Floor
The Worst Journey in the World by Ellen Back
Trouble in Lancashire by Igor Blimey
Try and Try Again by Percy Vere
Understanding Computers by Mike Rochips

Boredom

Why did the plank of wood complain of having nothing to do?
It was board.

A cheerful old bear at the zoo
Could always find something to do.
When it bored him to go
On a walk to and fro,
He reversed it and walked fro and to.

What's the difference between a fisherman and a bored student?
One baits his hooks, while the other hates his books.

Did you hear about the unemployed man who took up meditation?
He was bored with sitting around all day doing nothing.

'I have had a perfectly wonderful evening – but this wasn't it.' *(Groucho Marx)*

Boxing

Can an orange box?
No, but a baked bean can.

Can a shoe box?
No, but a tin can.

What do boxers drink?
Punch.

What is the difference between a boxer and a man with a cold?
One knows his blows and the other blows his nose.

Burglars

What do you call two burglars?
A pair of knickers.

Did you hear about the burglar who fell into a concrete mixer?
Now he's a hardened criminal.

Did you hear about the burglar who stole a calendar?
He got twelve months.

Did you hear about the burglar who stole a lamp?
He got a light sentence.

A burglar is robbing a house when he is distracted by a voice saying, 'Jesus is watching you.' He looks wildly about him and realizes it is just a pet parrot talking. 'What's your name?' he asks the bird. 'Moses.' The burglar guffaws with laughter. 'Moses? What kind of person would call their parrot Moses?' The parrot shrugs. 'The same kind of person who calls his Rottweiler Jesus.'

My mum and dad are in the iron and steel business. She does the ironing and he does the stealing.

'Wake up, dear, there's a burglar downstairs in the kitchen eating that pie I made this afternoon! Ring 999!'
'Shall I ask for the police or an ambulance?'

Why did the burglar have a shower before leaving?
He wanted to make a clean getaway.

Why did the thief saw the legs off his bed?
He wanted to lie low.

Did you hear about the French burglar who ran out of petrol as he made his getaway after stealing paintings from the Louvre?
He had no Monet to buy Degas to make the Van Gogh.

'Now then, Nobbs, we can produce six people who say they saw you stealing the diamonds!'
'That's nothing – I can produce millions who didn't.'

'We had gay burglars the other night. They broke in and rearranged the furniture.' *(Robin Williams)*

Old burglars never die, they just steal away.

See also **Courts of law**; **Criminals**; **Police officers**; **Prison**.

Business

Why did the balloon factory close?
There was a fall in inflation.

Did you hear what happened to the paper company?
It folded.

Did you hear about the man who made a great success in
the cement business?
He was a great mixer.

A businessman was late for an appointment. As he hurried
out of his hotel he called to the commissionaire: 'You
there – call me a taxi!' The commissionaire tapped his cap:
'You're a taxi!'

Why did the businessman sleep with a clock under his
pillow?
He wanted to work overtime.

'There's only one honest way to make money.'
'What's that?'
'I thought you wouldn't know it!'

'The man who invented the zip fastener was today
honoured with a lifetime peerage. He will now be known
as the Lord of the Flies.' *(Ronnie Barker)*

'So I was in my car, and I was driving along, and my boss
rang up and he said, "You've been promoted." And I
swerved. And then he rang up a second time and said,
"You've been promoted again." And I swerved again. He
rang up a third time and said, "You're managing director."
And I went into a tree. And a policeman came up and said,
"What happened to you?" And I said, "I careered off the
road." ' *(Tim Vine)*

See also **Accountants**; **Punctuality**; **Taxation**; **Work**.

Butterflies

Why couldn't the butterfly go to the dance?
It was a mothball.

What did the worm say to the caterpillar?
'Where did you get that fur coat?'

What are caterpillars frightened of?
Dogerpillars.

What does a caterpillar do on New Year's Day?
It turns over a new leaf.

What did the caterpillar say to the other caterpillar when a
butterfly passed overhead?
'You'll never get me up in one of those things.'

See also **Moths**.

Calendars

Why was the calendar so anxious?
Its days were numbered.

Why are soldiers tired on 1 April?
They've just had a 31-day March.

What are the four seasons?
Salt, pepper, mustard and vinegar.

What season is it when you are on a trampoline?
Spring time.

What is the longest night of the year?
A fortnight.

Which days of the week start with T?
Tuesday, Thursday, today and tomorrow.

How many seconds are there in a year?
Twelve: second of January, second of February . . .

See also **Time**.

Callers

'Who was that at the door?'
'A man with a drum.'
'Well, tell him to beat it.'

'Who was that at the door?'
'A man with a wooden leg.'
'Well, tell him to hop it.'

'Who was that at the door?'
'A man selling bees.'
'Well, tell him to buzz off.'

'Who was that at the door?'
'The Invisible Man.'
'Well, tell him I can't see him.'

See also **Knock**, **knock**.

Camels

Why was the camel unhappy?
It had the hump.

What do you call a camel with three humps?
Humphrey.

What do you call a camel with no humps?
Humphrey.

How do you get down from a camel?
You don't. You get down from a duck.

What do camels wear in the jungle?
Camelflage.

A man buys a camel and is told that it obeys three words of command. To make it walk he must say, 'Few.' To make it run he must say, 'Many.' To make it stop he must say, 'Amen!' He hands over the money and decides to try the beast out right away. He mounts the animal and when he calls out, 'Few!' the camel dutifully sets off at a walk. When he shouts, 'Many!' the camel breaks into a run. Unfortunately, it aims straight for the edge of a cliff and, to his horror, the man realizes he has forgotten the word to make it stop. As they hurtle towards the precipice the man utters a last desperate prayer: 'Oh Lord, get me out of this! Amen!' On hearing the magic word, the camel suddenly stops, right on the brink of the drop. Shuddering with relief, the man mops the sweat from his brow and catches his breath. 'Phew – aaaaaargh!'

What do you get if you cross a cow with a camel?
Lumpy milkshakes.

Cannibals

What kind of beans do cannibals like?
Human beans.

What sort of soup do cannibals like?
One with plenty of body in it.

What did the cannibal get when he was late for dinner?
The cold shoulder.

What happened when the cannibal sailed on the *QE2*?
He asked the waiter for the passenger list.

Why was the cannibal expelled from school?
He kept buttering up the teacher.

What game do cannibals like to play?
Swallow my leader.

Why did the cannibal live on his own?
He was fed up with other people.

How can you help a starving cannibal?
Give him a hand.

What did the cannibal say when he was full?
'I couldn't eat another mortal!'

Did you hear about the cannibal who went on a diet?
He ate only pygmies.

What did the cannibal say when he came home and found
his wife chopping up a python and a pygmy?
'Oh, no, not snake and pygmy pie again!'

What happened to the cannibal lion?
He had to swallow his pride.

What does a cannibal call a skateboarder?
Meals on wheels.

I like kids, but I don't think I could manage a whole one.

Why don't cannibals eat weathermen?
Because they give them wind.

Why did the cannibals welcome the first missionaries?
They gave them their first taste of Christianity.

Did you hear about the missionary who was carried off by
cannibals?
He got into a real stew.

Two cannibals are eating a clown when one turns to the
other and says, 'Does this taste funny to you?'

A newspaper reporter is captured by cannibals, who
immediately pop him into a cauldron. 'What was your
job?' one of the cannibals politely inquires. 'I was a
sub-editor.' 'Congratulations,' the cannibal replies, 'you're
about to become editor-in-chief.'

Two cannibals are eating dinner when one says, 'I hate my
sister.'
'Well,' says the other, 'just eat the noodles.'

What should you call a cannibal who eats his mother's
sister?
An aunt-eater.

Did you hear about the cannibal who ate his
mother-in-law?
She still didn't agree with him.

Who do cannibals like their daughters to marry?
Edible bachelors.

Why was the cannibal thrown out of the wedding
reception?
He toasted the bride and groom.

Did you hear about that meal I had in the cannibal restaurant?
It cost an arm and a leg.

Teacher Julie, what is a cannibal?
Julie I don't know.
Teacher Well, if you ate your parents, what would you be?
Julie An orphan.

'A cannibal is a guy who goes into a restaurant and orders the waiter.' *(Jack Benny)*

Cars

When is a car not a car?
When it turns into a side street.

When is a car like a frog?
When it's being toad.

What happened when the car saw a ghost?
It had a nervous breakdown.

What do you call songs about cars?
Cartoons.

What has four wheels and flies?
A garbage truck.

How do you fit five elephants into a car?
Two in the front, two in the back and the other in the glove compartment.

What's the most dangerous part of a car?
The nut behind the wheel.

How did the soldier get back into his car after losing his keys?
He rubbed the lock with his khaki trousers.

An old lady bought a foreign-made car with a rear engine. When she took one of her friends out for a ride the car broke down. The women got out and opened the bonnet. 'Oh dear,' said the old lady's friend, 'someone's pinched your engine!' 'Don't worry,' the old lady replied, 'I've got a spare in the boot.'

I couldn't repair your brakes, so I made your horn louder.

What kind of bus crosses the ocean?
A Columbus.

What did the big bus say to the little bus?
'You're too young to drive.'

*See also **Accidents**; **Motorists**; **Traffic wardens**.*

Caterpillars *See **Butterflies**.*

Cats

Why do cats have furry coats?
Because they would look silly in plastic macs.

What do cats eat for breakfast?
Mice crispies. Or mewsli.

How do you know if a cat has eaten a duck?
He's a little down in the mouth.

What do you call a cat that has just eaten a duck?
A duck-filled fatty puss.

How is cat food sold?
Purr can.

What dessert do cats like best?
Catameringue.

What do French cats eat?
Chocolate mousse.

What do Chinese cats eat?
Egg fried mice.

What kind of cats love water?
Octopusses.

Did you hear about the cat who swallowed a ball of wool?
She had mittens.

What do you call a cat with no legs?
Dog food.

How do you know if your cat's got a bad cold?
From the catarrh.

Why did the cat join the Red Cross?
She wanted to be a first-aid kit.

Why are cats longer in the evening than they are in the
morning?
Because they are let out at night and taken in in the
morning.

How do cats keep up with current affairs?
They read the mewspapers.

'A tomcat hijacked a plane, stuck a pistol into the pilot's ribs and demanded: "Take me to the canaries."'
(Bob Monkhouse)

Which cats purr the most?
Purrsians.

Why are cats such good singers?
They're very mewsical.

What kind of cats live in Poland?
Polecats.

What do you call a posh puss?
An aristocat.

What should you put a cat statue on?
A caterpillar.

'My dog is so clever he can bark up to ten.'
'I know. My cat told me.'

'Did you put the cat out?'
'I didn't know it was on fire.'

What looks like half a cat?
The other half.

What is the difference between a cat and a comma?
One has claws at the end of its paws and the other has a pause at the end of its clause.

A motorist accidentally runs over an old lady's cat. He finds the cat's address on its collar and knocks on the old lady's door. 'I'm sorry,' he says, 'but I've run over your cat and killed it. I would be happy to replace it.' 'Great,' says the old lady, 'but how are you at catching mice?'

What do you get if you cross a cat with a lemon?
A sour puss.

What do you get if you cross a cat with a Pekingese?
A Peking Tom.

What do you get if you cross a cat with an octagon?
An octopus.

What do you get if you cross a cat with a tree?
A catalogue.

Chickens

Why did the chicken go red?
It was henbarrassed.

Why was the chicken sent home from school?
It used fowl language.

Why did the chicken get detention?
For playing practical yolks.

What do chicken families do on Saturday afternoon?
They go on peck-nics.

Which day of the week do chickens hate most?
Fry-day.

What do roosters use to get up in the morning?
An alarm cluck.

What is a lazy cockerel called?
A cock-a-doodle-don't.

What do iron chickens do at the end of the day?
They come home to rust.

If fruit comes from a fruit tree, what tree does a chicken grow on?
A poultry.

Where do tough chickens come from?
Hard-boiled eggs.

What happens if a chicken eats gunpowder?
It lays hand gren-eggs.

What happens if you drop a hand gren-egg?
It eggs-plodes.

What kind of bird lays electric eggs?
A battery hen.

How do chickens encourage their young?
They egg them on.

Why did the chick disappoint his mother?
He wasn't what he was cracked up to be.

What goes 'cluck-cluck-boom'?
A chicken in a minefield.

Why did the chicken cross the road?
To get to the other side.

Why didn't the chicken cross the road?
He was chicken.

Why did the chicken cross the road with a gun and a pair
of scissors?
It wanted to shoot across the road and cut the corners.

Why did the one-eyed chicken cross the road?
To get to the Bird's Eye shop.

Why did the indecisive chicken cross the road?
To get to the other side. Well, no, to go shopping. No, not
that either . . .

Why did the chicken cross the road, roll in the mud and
cross the road again?
Because it was a dirty double-crosser.

What do you call a chicken crossing the road?
Poultry in motion.

Why did the chicken cross the playground?
To get to the other slide.

Why did the turkey cross the road?
To prove he wasn't chicken.

Why did the chewing-gum cross the road?
It was stuck to the chicken's foot.

What do you get if you cross a chicken with a dog?
Pooched eggs.

What do you get if you cross a chicken with a
cement-mixer?
A bricklayer.

Children

Why did the little boy put lipstick on his head?
He wanted to make up his mind.

A vicar spots a small boy struggling to reach a door
knocker and kindly knocks on the door for him. 'Thanks,'
says the little boy. 'Now, run like mad!'

A police officer finds a small boy who has got separated
from his father at a football match. 'What's your dad like?'
the police officer asks in a kindly voice. 'Beer and women,'
the boy replies.

There are three ways to get things done. Do them yourself,
pay someone else to do them, or forbid your kids doing
them.

See also **Families**; **Parents**; **School**.

Christmas

'Knock, knock.'
'Who's there?'
'Mary.'
'Mary who?'
'Mary Christmas!'

What king do you see every Christmas?
A stock-king.

What did the fireman's wife get for Christmas?
A ladder in her stocking.

Why did the old lady knit her grandson three socks for Christmas?
Because she heard he had grown another foot.

What is Father Christmas's telephone number?
O O O.

What are Father Christmas's helpers called?
Subordinate clauses.

Why was Father Christmas's helper feeling glum?
He had low elf-esteem.

What do you call someone who is frightened of Father Christmas?
Santaclaustrophobic.

'Santa Claus has the right idea – visit people only once a year.' *(Victor Borge)*

Clairvoyants *See* **Psychics**.

Clocks and watches

Why can't clocks keep secrets?
Because time will tell.

Why did the clock go to the doctor?
It was feeling run-down.

Did you hear about the hungry clock?
It went back four seconds.

A man goes into a shop and asks a sales assistant, 'Do you sell potato clocks?' 'Potato clocks?' replies the assistant. 'I'm not sure I know what you mean.' 'It's my boss,' explains the man. 'He keeps telling me I'm always late for work at nine o'clock, but there wouldn't be a problem if I got a potato clock.'

What did the Leaning Tower of Pisa say to Big Ben? 'If you've got the time, I've got the inclination.'

What did the big hand say to the little hand? 'I'll be back in an hour.'

'Doctor, doctor, I keep thinking I'm a clock!' 'There's no cause for alarm.'

'Doctor, doctor, I still think I'm a clock!' 'Don't get so wound up.'

'Doctor, doctor, I think I'm a Swiss clock!' 'You're going cuckoo.'

'Knock, knock.'
'Who's there?'
'Juno.'
'Juno who?'
'Juno what the time is? My watch is broken.'

Why didn't the idiot throw his broken watch away? Because it was right twice a day.

What will watches be called in the future? Future-wrist-tick.

See also **Time**.

Clothing

I went to buy some camouflage trousers the other day but I couldn't find any.

What do you get if you cross a pair of trousers with a telephone?
Bell-bottoms.

Why was the belt arrested?
For holding up a pair of trousers.

What has four legs and flies?
Two pairs of jeans.

When is a chair like a dress?
When it is satin.

Why did the blonde keep her dresses in the fridge?
She liked to have something cool to slip into in the evenings.

'Do your socks have holes?'
'Certainly not!'
'Then how do you get your feet in?'

'You're wearing differently coloured socks. One is pink with green stripes and the other is yellow with red spots.'
'I know. And I've got another pair just like these at home.'

Did you hear about the boy who put on a clean pair of socks every day?
By the end of the week he couldn't get his shoes on.

What's the difference between a camera and a sock?
A camera takes four toes and a sock takes five toes.

What did the tie say to the hat?
'You go on ahead and I'll hang around.'

What bow can't be tied?
A rainbow.

What do you get if you cross a black hat with a rocket?
A fast bowler.

What wears a long coat and pants in the summer?
A dog.

How can you get four suits for a pound?
Buy a pack of cards.

What do you get if you cross a suit with a biscuit?
A smart cookie.

'Can I try on that blue suit in the window?'
'No, use the changing cubicle like everyone else.'

Why do people laugh up their sleeves?
Because that's where their funny bone is.

Where does Tarzan buy his clothes?
At jungle sales.

'That girl looks like Helen Green.'
'She looks even worse in red.'

'And the back of his anorak was leaping up and down, and
people were chucking money to him. I said, "Do you earn a
living doing that?" He said, "Yes, this is my livelihood." '
(Tommy Cooper)

'I spilt some stain remover on my sleeve. How do you get that out?' *(Bob Monkhouse)*

See also **Underwear**.

College See **Higher education**.

Comedians

How do comedians send messages to each other?
By tee-hee mail.

How did the comedian murder his wife?
He joked her to death.

What do you call an out-of-work jester?
Nobody's fool.

How did the comedian go down at the werewolves' party?
He had them howling in the aisles.

Who tells chicken jokes?
Comedihens.

'When I first said I wanted to be a comedian, everybody laughed. They're not laughing now.' *(Bob Monkhouse)*

Computers

What happens if you get a gigabyte?
It megahertz.

What do computers eat when they get hungry?
Chips.

What can you clean in a *www.ashing* machine?
Net curtains.

Which key on the computer do astronauts use most?
The spacebar.

How do you know if you are a computing novice?
You cannot find the 'any' key.

How can you tell when a teacher has been using a
computer?
There is correction fluid all over the screen.

What is the best way to wreck a computer?
Let a grown-up use it.

What do you get if you cross an elephant with a PC?
A computer with a really big memory.

'A computer once beat me at chess, but it was no match
for me at kick-boxing.' *(Emo Philips)*

Cooking

How do you make an apple puff?
Chase it round the garden.

What do you get if you cross the white of an egg with a
pound of gunpowder?
A boom-meringue.

What were the last words of the egg in the monastery?
'Out of the frying pan, into the friar!'

Where can you learn how to make ice cream?
Sundae school.

What's the difference between school dinners and fresh manure?
School dinners are cold.

How do they keep flies out of the school cafeteria?
They let them taste the food.

Why are cooks cruel?
Because they beat eggs, whip cream and batter fish.

How did the chef save the life of a sick woman?
He gave her the quiche of life.

Did you hear about the famous chef who was cremated yesterday?
It took 20 minutes at gas mark 6.

I wouldn't call Mum's gravy thick but when I try to stir it the house spins round.

Did you hear about the students who never cooked a single meal the whole time they were at college?
Every recipe they looked at began the same way: 'Take a clean dish.'

'I'm not saying my wife's a bad cook, but she uses a smoke alarm as a timer.' *(Bob Monkhouse)*

*See also **Food**; **Restaurants**.*

Courts of law

Clerk Prisoner at the bar, how do you plead, guilty or not guilty?
Accused How can I tell till I've heard the evidence?

Accused As the Lord is my judge, I am not guilty.
Judge He's not, I am, you are, six months.

Judge Prisoner at the bar, you have been brought here for drinking.
Accused Great! Mine's a pint!

Judge You have been found not guilty of robbery and can leave this court without a stain on your character.
Accused Great! Does that mean I can keep the money?

See also **Criminals**; **Executions**; **Judges**; **Police officers**; **Prison**.

Cowboys

'Knock, knock.'
'Who's there?'
'Ya.'
'Ya who?'
'I didn't know you were a cowboy.'

Why do cowboys pitch their tents on top of stoves?
So they can have a home on the range.

A cowboy rode into town on Friday, stayed for four days and left on Friday. How come?
Friday was the name of his horse.

A three-legged dog limps into a Wild West saloon. He sidles up to the bar and growls, 'I'm looking for the man who shot my paw.'

Who has eight guns and terrorizes the ocean?
Billy the Squid.

Cows

'Knock, knock.'
'Who's there?'
'Cows.'
'Cows who?'
'Cows go moo not who.'

Why do cows lie down when it's cold?
To keep each udder warm.

What do cows produce when it's hot?
Evaporated milk.

Why did the cow jump over the moon?
Because the farmer's hands were cold.

How do you make a milkshake?
Creep up on a cow and shout, 'Boo!'

Mary had a bionic cow,
It lived on safety pins.
And every time she milked that cow
The milk came out in tins.

Why do cows never have any money?
The farmers milk them dry.

Why do cows like being told jokes?
Because they like to be amoosed.

Why did the cow cross the road?
To get to the udder side.

What do you call a cow that eats grass?
A lawn-mooer.

What has four legs and goes 'Boo'?
A cow with a cold.

What do you call a man standing in cow muck?
An incowpoop.

What do you get if you crawl under a cow?
A pat on the head.

Where do cows go on holiday?
Moo York.

Why do cows have bells round their necks?
In case their horns don't work.

Two cows are standing in a field. One turns to the other and says, 'Moo.' 'Hey,' replies the other, 'I was about to say that!'

What goes 'moo, baa, oink, woof, quack'?
A cow that can speak five languages.

What do you call a herd of cows that can't stop giggling?
Laughing stock.

How does a farmer count his cows?
He uses a cowculator.

What sort of maths are cows best at?
Cowculus.

What did one Highland cow say to the other?
'Och, aye the moo!'

Where might you see a prehistoric cow?
In a mooseum.

Where do cows go on Saturday night?
To the moovies.

Why did the bull rush?
Because it saw the cow slip.

A man found himself in a field with a dangerous-looking bull. When he spotted the farmer on the other side of the fence he called out, 'Is that bull safe?' 'Sure,' said the farmer, 'but I don't think you are.'

Did you hear what happened when the cows got out of the field?
Udder chaos.

What romantic song do cows like best?
'When I fall in love, it will be for heifer.'

Two cows are waiting to be milked. One turns to the other and says, 'Are you worried about all this mad cow disease?' 'Why should that worry me?' says the other. 'I'm a chicken.'

What do you get if you cross a cow with a chicken?
Roost beef.

Crabs

Why did the crab blush?
Because the sea weed.

Why was the crab arrested?
It pinched something.

Why didn't the crab let the other sea creatures play with its toys?
Because it was shellfish.

How do lobsters travel to work?
By taxi crab.

See also **Shellfish**.

Cricket

Which birds do cricketers fear most?
Ducks.

Why did the fish lose their cricket match with the sharks?
They let the goldfish bowl.

What sport do insects like best?
Cricket.

An expectant father rings the hospital to find out how his pregnant wife is getting along, but accidentally dials the cricket results service instead. When he asks about the latest progress he is told, 'We've got three out and hope to get the rest out by lunch. The last one was a duck.'

Criminals

There once was a man name of Finnigin
Who broke out of gaol to sinnigin.
He broke laws by the dozen,
Even stole from his cousin,
Now the gaol he broke out of, he's innigin.

A bank robber points two fingers at the bank manager and says, 'This is a muck-up!' The bank manager looks confused. 'Don't you mean a stick-up?' 'No,' says the bank robber, 'I forgot my gun.'

A young man rushes up to a passer-by in the street and asks urgently, 'Have you seen a policeman near here?' 'Sorry, no,' the passer-by replies. The young man pulls out a gun. 'Then give me all your money.'

What do you call a person who steals meat from a butcher's shop?
A choplifter.

What do you call a thief who steals pigs?
A hamburglar.

'Doctor, Doctor, I can't help stealing!'
'Have you taken anything for it?'

Newsflash: A lorryload of filing cabinets and document folders has been stolen tonight. The police believe it is the work of organized crime.

Did you hear about the unluckiest criminal in the world? He made a deathbed confession, then got better.

'Arnold Crump, a six-foot-nine-inches, ham-fisted, hairy drunk with a short temper, bad breath, acne, dandruff and fleas, was named by Scotland Yard today as Britain's most unwanted man.' *(Ronnie Barker)*

See also **Burglars**; **Courts of law**; **Executions**; **Gangsters**; **Police officers**; **Prison**.

Crocodiles

What card game do crocodiles like best?
Snap.

What do you call a sick crocodile?
An illigator.

A man takes his pet crocodile with him to watch a film at the cinema. 'I didn't think I'd ever see a crocodile in here watching the film!' says the usher. 'Neither did I,' says the man. 'He hated the book!'

What do you get if you cross a parrot with a crocodile?
Something that bites your head off and says, 'Who's a pretty boy, then?'

D

Dancing

Did you hear about the stupid tap dancer?
He fell in the sink.

What dance do tin-openers do?
The can-can.

To what kind of dance do you invite people you don't like?
An avoidance.

What is the dance capital of the USA?
San Frandisco.

What do overweight ballerinas wear?
Three-threes.

What ballet do pigs like best?
Swine Lake.

How do hens dance?
Chick to chick.

What dance do ducks like?
The quackstep.

'I grew up with six brothers. That's how I learned to dance
– waiting for the bathroom.' *(Bob Hope)*

'I could dance with you until the cows come home – on second thoughts, I'd rather dance with the cows until you come home.' *(Groucho Marx)*

Dating

What did the boy candle say to the girl candle?
'Let's go out together.'

Fork Who was that ladle I saw you with last night?
Spoon That was no ladle. That was my knife.

She frowned and called him Mr
Because he boldly Kr
And so in spite
That very night
This Mr Kr Sr.

'If I held you any closer I'd be on the other side of you.'
(Groucho Marx)

Did you hear about the man whose girlfriend said he should be more affectionate?
He got two girlfriends.

'Have you had any replies to your advert for a husband in the lonely hearts column?'
'Yes, fourteen. But they all say the same thing.'
'What?'
'You can have mine!'

'My sister is engaged to an Irish bloke.'
'Oh, really?'
'No – O'Reilly.'

'I could marry anyone I please.'
'So why don't you?'
'I haven't pleased anyone yet.'

'Whoever named it necking was a poor judge of anatomy.'
(Groucho Marx)

'My father told me all about the birds and the bees, the
liar – I went steady with a woodpecker till I was
twenty-one.' *(Bob Hope)*

See also **Love**; **Marriage**; **Sex**.

Death

Death is God's way of telling you to slow down.

Die? That's the last thing I shall do!

'Either he's dead or my watch has stopped.' *(Groucho Marx)*

'Doctor, doctor, I'm at death's door!'
'Don't worry, I'll pull you through it.'

Why did they have to put a fence round the graveyard?
Because everyone was dying to get in.

A man is visiting the cemetery when his attention is
drawn to another man kneeling at a grave. The man keeps
repeating, 'Why did you have to die? Why did you have to
die?' After several minutes of this the first man approaches
him and says, 'Excuse me, I don't wish to interfere, but for
whom do you mourn so deeply? A close relative, perhaps?'
The second man wipes his eyes then replies, 'My wife's
first husband.'

'I want to die like my father, peacefully in his sleep, not screaming and terrified, like his passengers.' *(Bob Monkhouse)*

During the war it was often said that you would only be hit by a bomb if it had your name written on it. Which was bad luck on Mr and Mrs Doodlebug.

'I don't want to achieve immortality through my work – I want to achieve it through not dying.' *(Woody Allen)*

What do you find in the middle of a graveyard?
The dead centre.

'It's not that I'm afraid to die, I just don't want to be there when it happens.' *(Woody Allen)*

See also **Funerals**; **Ghosts**; **Suicide**; **Undertakers**.

Deer

'Have you heard the one about the three deer?'
'No.'
'Dear, dear, dear . . .'

What do you call a deer with no eyes?
No idea (eye-deer).

What do you call a deer with no eyes and no legs?
Still no idea.

What is the wettest animal in the world?
A reindeer.

Why are fully-grown reindeer so expensive?
Because they are big bucks.

Dentists

Why are dentists unhappy?
Because they are always looking down in the mouth.

What was the name of the Scottish dentist?
Phil McAvity.

What's the best time to visit the dentist?
Tooth-hurty.

What are dental X-rays known as?
Tooth pics.

'So I went to the dentist. He said, "Say Aaah." I said,
"Why?" He said, "My dog's died." ' *(Tim Vine)*

Patient Excuse me, but how much are you going to charge
me for extracting this tooth?
Dentist Fifty pounds.
Patient Fifty pounds for a few minutes' work?
Dentist I can do it slowly if you prefer.

What is the dentist's favourite musical instrument?
A tuba toothpaste.

'Now, most dentists' chairs go up and down, don't they?
The one I was in went back and forwards. I thought, "This
is unusual." And the dentist said to me, "Mr Vine, get out
of the filing cabinet." ' *(Tim Vine)*

Old dentists never die, they just lose their pull.

See also **Teeth**.

Dictionary definitions

Abundance A dance in a bakery.
Anarachnophobia Fear of anoraks.
Apex A gorilla's old girlfriend.
Blazer A jacket that is always on fire.
Blood brother A vampire's relative.
Bulldozer A sleepy male cow.
Buttress A female goat.
Carpet A dog that lives in a car.
Catastrophe First prize in a cat show.
Denial A river in Egypt.
Fjord A Norwegian car.
Fortune A singing quartet.
Grammar A female grandparent.
Hail Hard-boiled rain.
Hypnotism Rheumatism of the hip.
Inkling A small pen.
Jubilant A celebrating insect.
Juggernaut A jug of nothing.
Kindred Fear of relatives.
Kipper A sleepy fish.
Lavish Like a lavatory.
Myth A female moth.
Net Holes tied together with string.
Octopus An eight-sided cat.
Offal Something dreadful.
Optical Itching eyes.
Overture A person who takes a long time eating.

Polygon A dead parrot.
Rugged Seated on a mat.
Syntax A collection in church.
Tangent A gentleman with a suntan.
Viper Used to clean vindows.
Zeal An enthusiastic sea mammal.

Diets

Did you hear about the elephant that went on a crash diet?
He wrecked three cars, two buses and a fire engine.

'How can I lose 12 pounds of ugly fat?'
'Cut your head off.'

'I'm on a whisky diet. I've lost three days already.' *(Tommy Cooper)*

What makes the Tower of Pisa lean?
It's careful what it eats.

'My wife lost two stone swimming last year. I don't
know how. I tied them round her neck tight enough.'
(Les Dawson)

I used to be thin.
Now I'm thinner.
So would you be
With our school dinner.

Did you hear about the sword-swallower who went on a
diet?
He has pins and needles.

There was an old fellow named Green
Who grew so abnormally lean,
And flat, and compressed,
That his back touched his chest,
And sideways he couldn't be seen.

There once was a lady named Lynn
Who was so uncommonly thin
That when she assayed
To drink lemonade,
She slipped through the straw and fell in.

There once was a baker named Fred
Whose success never went to his head.
Instead of just looking,
He ate all his cooking,
So it went to his waistline instead.

Old dieticians never die, they just waist away.

See also **Anatomy**; **Exercise**; **Food**; **Health**.

Dinosaurs

What do you call a one-eyed dinosaur?
Do-you-think-he-saw-us?

Why did the dinosaur cross the road?
Because chickens hadn't been invented yet.

How did the dinosaurs pass their exams?
With extinction.

What came after the dinosaurs?
Their tails.

Divorce

What do a hurricane, a fire and a divorce have in common?
They are all ways you can lose your home.

Did you hear about the woman who divorced her husband because he had a bad memory?
Every time he met a pretty woman he forgot he was married.

A woman is yelling at her husband, 'You're going to be sorry! I'm going to leave you!' 'Make up your mind!' replies the husband. 'Which one is it going to be?'

Have you heard about the new 'Divorce Barbie'?
It comes with all of Ken's stuff.

See also **Husbands and wives**; **Marriage**.

Doctor, doctor

'Doctor, doctor, I feel like a pair of curtains!'
'Pull yourself together, man.'

'Doctor, doctor, I feel like a bell!'
'Take these and if they don't work, give me a ring.'

'Doctor, doctor, I feel like a pack of cards!'
'Stop shuffling around and I'll deal with you later.'

'Doctor, doctor, I think I'm a spoon!'
'Sit over there and don't stir.'

'Doctor, doctor, I think I'm a bridge!'
'What's come over you, man?'
'A lorry, two cars and a bus!'

'Doctor, doctor, I think I'm a dustbin!'
'Don't talk rubbish.'

'Doctor, doctor, I think I need glasses!'
'This is a fish and chip shop.'

'Doctor, doctor, I keep seeing double!'
'Take a seat.'
'Which one?'

'Doctor, doctor, I keep thinking I'm a wigwam and a tepee!'
'Calm down – you're two tents.'

'Doctor, doctor, I keep thinking there's two of me!'
'One at a time, please.'

'Doctor, doctor, I can see into the future!'
'When did this start happening?'
'Next Tuesday.'

'Doctor, doctor, I've got a little stye.'
'Get a little pig.'

'Doctor, doctor, can you give me something for my liver?'
'How about some onions?'

'Doctor, doctor, I've just been attacked by a six-foot-tall insect!'
'Yes, there's a nasty bug going round.'

'Doctor, doctor, I keep seeing images of Donald Duck and Mickey Mouse!'
'How long have you been having these Disney spells?'

'Doctor, doctor, will this cream clear up my spots?'
'I never make rash promises.'

'Doctor, doctor, I'm getting smaller and smaller every day!'
'I can't see you until Friday.'
'But I'll have shrunk even more by then!'
'Well, you'll just have to be a little patient.'

'Doctor, doctor, I've only got fifty-nine seconds to live!'
'Wait just a minute and I'll be right with you.'

'Doctor, doctor, everybody ignores me!'
'Next, please.'

'Doctor, doctor, I have a lot of trouble making friends, you stupid idiot.'

'Doctor, doctor, I can't feel my legs!'
'I know you can't, I've cut your arms off.'

'Doctor, doctor, I can't stop clucking and it frightens me!'
'Don't be such a chicken.'

'Doctor, doctor, I've got some lettuce sticking out of my ear!'
'That's just the tip of the iceberg.'

'Doctor, doctor, I've swallowed my pen!'
'Use a pencil instead.'

'Doctor, doctor, I've swallowed a whistle!'
'Be quiet, and don't let me hear another peep out of you.'

'Doctor, doctor, I've swallowed a roll of film!'
'Sit in a darkened room and see what develops.'

'Doctor, doctor, my little boy's swallowed a bullet!'
'Don't point him at me!'

'Doctor, doctor, I can't control my aggression.'
'How long have you had this problem?'
'Who wants to know?'

'Doctor, doctor, I think I'm suffering from déjà vu!'
'Didn't I see you yesterday?'

'Doctor, doctor, when I press with my finger here it hurts, and here, and here, and here . . .'
'You've broken your finger.'

'Doctor, doctor, I keep thinking I'm a doctor.'
'I must stop talking to myself!'

Doctors

'Knock, knock.'
'Who's there?'
'Doctor.'
'Doctor who?'
'That's right.'

A man walks into the doctor's. 'We haven't seen you here lately,' the doctor observes. 'Well,' says the man, 'I've been ill . . .'

Doctor Nurse, we need to get these people to hospital.
Nurse What is it?

Doctor A big building full of doctors, but that's not important now!

Doctor I'm sorry to tell you you're dying.
Patient How long have I got?
Doctor Ten . . .
Patient Ten what? Ten months? Ten weeks?
Doctor Ten, nine, eight, seven . . .

A woman went to see the doctor about a pimple on her face. It had a tree growing out of it as well as some bushes and a picnic table and four chairs. 'Don't worry,' said the doctor. 'It's just a beauty spot.'

'Mr Jones, I have some good news and some bad news. Which would you like first?'
'The bad news, doctor.'
'Your legs will have to come off.'
'The good news?'
'The man in the next bed wants to buy your slippers.'

'Now, Mrs Smith, I want you to take one of these tablets three times a day.'
'How can I take it more than once?'

Why do surgeons wear masks in the operating theatre?
So no one will know who they are if they make a mistake.

Doctor I have good news and bad news.
Patient What's the bad news?
Doctor We cut off the wrong leg.
Patient What's the good news?
Doctor The bad leg is getting better.

Did you hear what happened when the plastic surgeon went sunbathing?
He melted.

Doctor I have good news and bad news. Which would you like first?
Patient What's the bad news?
Doctor You have only twenty-four hours to live.
Patient And the good news?
Doctor See that gorgeous blonde over there? She's my girlfriend.

Doctor I have good news and bad news. The good news is that you're not a hypochondriac.

Doctor Have your eyes been checked?
Patient No, they've always been brown.

Why do doctors make poor kidnappers?
No one can read their ransom demands.

There was a faith healer of Deal
Who said: 'Although pain is not real,
When I sit on a pin,
And puncture my skin,
I dislike what I fancy I feel.'

'My doctor gave me six months to live but when I couldn't pay the bill he gave me six months more.'
(Walter Matthau)

Old doctors never die, they just lose their patience.

See also **Doctor**, **doctor**; **Hospitals**; **Ill-health**.

Dogs

What did the dog say when it sat on some sandpaper?
'Ruff!'

Why do dogs always put their puppies back in their basket?
Because they know they shouldn't leave their litter lying around.

Why are puppies good at DIY?
They like doing little jobs around the house.

Which dogs are the cleanest?
Shampoodles.

Which dogs are always in a hurry?
Dashhunds.

What kind of dog travels the world?
A jet-setter.

How did the little Scottie dog feel when he saw a monster?
Terrier-fied.

Where would you find a dog with no legs?
Right where you left him.

What kind of dog has no head, no legs and no tail?
A hot dog.

Did you hear about the dog who went to see the flea circus?
He stole the show.

Did you hear about the Chihuahua that killed an Alsatian?
It got stuck in his throat and choked him.

What do you get if you cross a Rottweiler with a collie?
A dog that will bite your arm off then run to fetch help.

What has four legs and an arm?
A pit bull terrier.

What do you call a dog in jeans and a sweater?
A plain clothes police dog.

What is the difference between a well-dressed man and a dog?
The man wears a suit and the dog just pants.

Did you hear about the man who lost his dog?
He put an advert in the paper saying, 'Here, boy!'

Have you heard the story about the dog who went ten miles to pick up a stick?
It is a little far-fetched.

What dog keeps the best time?
A watch dog.

What is the difference between a hot dog and a cold dog?
One goes 'grrr' and the other goes 'brrr'.

What do you give a dog with a fever?
Mustard (it's the best thing for a hot dog).

What is the difference between a dog with rabies and a hot dog?
One bites the hand that feeds it and the other feeds the hand that bites it.

Dog owner My dog chases anyone on a skateboard. What should I do?
Vet Take away its skateboard.

How far can a dog chase a rabbit into a wood?
Only halfway – after that he is chasing the rabbit out of the wood.

'Have you ever seen a dog make a rabbit hutch?'
'No, but I've seen a fox make a chicken run.'

A man walks into a pub and is amazed to see a man playing chess with his dog. He watches the game for a while then feels he has to say something. 'Who would have believed it? That must be the smartest dog I've ever seen!' The dog's owner shakes his head. 'Nah, he's not so smart. I usually win.'

A man takes his dog and cat to a talent agent, hoping to start a career in show business. The dog plays the piano as the cat sings and the agent is duly impressed. 'That's amazing! We'll make a fortune!' 'Listen,' says the man, 'I don't want you to think I'm pulling the wool over your eyes. The cat can't actually sing at all.' The agent looks crestfallen. 'The truth is,' the man continues, 'the dog's a ventriloquist.'

A man goes into a pet shop and buys a talking dog for £20. He then shows the dog to his friends and challenges them: 'I bet everyone £20 this dog can talk.' His friends all take the bet, only to find that the dog will not utter a word, however hard it is encouraged, and the bewildered owner reluctantly has to pay up. He takes the dog home and says out loud that he will return the dog to the pet shop next day and demand his money back. 'Use your head,' pipes up the dog wearily, 'just think of the odds we'll get tomorrow!'

Did you hear about the man who spent all afternoon trying to go up the escalator in the department store? The sign said 'Dogs must be carried' and it took him hours to find one.

Newsflash: Forty pedigree dogs have been stolen from some kennels. The police say they have no leads.

For sale: Pedigree bulldog. House-trained. Eats anything. Especially fond of children.

What is green and fluffy?
A seasick poodle.

What do you get if you cross a sheepdog with a bunch of daisies?
Collie-flowers.

What do you get if you cross a cocker spaniel with a poodle and a rooster?
A cockapoodledoo.

What do you get if you cross a dog with a cheetah?
A dog that chases cars and catches them.

What do you get if you cross a sheepdog with a plate of jelly?
Collie-wobbles.

'Doctor, doctor, I keep thinking I'm a dog!'
'How long have you felt like this?'
'Ever since I was a puppy.'

'Doctor, doctor, I think I'm a dog!'
'Take a seat.'
'I'm not allowed on the furniture.'

Donkeys

What parts of a donkey are the oldest?
Donkey's ears.

What do you call a donkey with three legs?
A wonkey.

What did the hungry donkey say when it had only thistles
to eat?
'Thistle have to do.'

How should you help a donkey in trouble?
Give it assistance.

What do you get if you cross a donkey with a jacket
potato?
A donkey jacket.

Dragons

Why did dragons like eating knights in armour?
They loved tinned food.

How did the polite dragon burn his fingers?
He covered his mouth when he coughed.

Why was the dragon full up?
He had Georged himself.

Why are dragons unhealthy?
Because they are always smoking.

Drink

What should you always take into the desert with you?
A thirst-aid kit.

'Have you heard the one about the three wells?'
'No.'
'Well, well, well . . .'

What do you call five bottles of lemonade?
A pop group.

What is the most popular drink in Australia?
Coca-koala.

Teacher Anne, name ten things with milk in them.
Anne Milkshake, tea, coffee, cocoa and – er – six cows.

See also **Alcohol**.

Ducks

What do you call a crate of ducks?
A box of quackers.

What goes 'quick, quick'?
A duck with hiccups.

Why don't ducks tell jokes when they are flying?
They might quack up.

Why did the duck run onto the football pitch?
The referee blew for a fowl.

What do you call a film about ducks?
A duckumentary.

Who stole the soap?
The robber duck.

How do you make a dumb blonde think she's a duck?
Tell her she's a duck.

What do you get if you cross a duck with a cat and a roadroller?
A duck-billed flatty puss.

What do you get if you cross a duck with a firework?
A firequacker.

Dumb blondes

What do you see when you look into a dumb blonde's eyes?
The back of her head.

How do you light up a dumb blonde's eyes?
Shine a torch in her ear.

How do you make a dumb blonde laugh on Monday morning?
Tell her a joke on Friday night.

Why was the dumb blonde so pleased when she finished her jigsaw puzzle after six months?
Because on the box it said '2–4 years'.

Why did the dumb blonde fall out of the window?
She was trying to iron her curtains.

A man on one side of a river sees a dumb blonde on the other side. He calls out: 'How do I get to the other side?' The dumb blonde calls back: 'You are on the other side!'

A dumb blonde decides to buy a new television. 'I would like to buy this TV,' she tells the sales assistant. 'I'm sorry, we don't sell to dumb blondes,' the man replies. The dumb blonde hurries home and dyes her hair, then comes back and again tells the sales assistant, 'I would like to buy this TV.' 'I'm sorry, we don't sell to dumb blondes,' he replies once more. Again the dumb blonde rushes home and this time adopts a full disguise, with a new haircut and new colour, new dress and sunglasses. A few days later she again approaches the sales assistant. 'I would like to buy this TV.' 'I'm sorry, we don't sell to dumb blondes,' he replies. 'How do you know I'm a dumb blonde?' exclaims the dumb blonde in exasperation. 'Because that's a microwave,' the man answers.

Nine dumb blondes and a brunette are holding on to the wings of an aircraft, which is beginning to lose height. One of the dumb blondes says that one of them will have to let go to save the others. The brunette delivers a heroic farewell speech and all the dumb blondes clap.

How do you get a one-armed dumb blonde out of a tree?
Wave to her.

Did you hear about the dumb blonde who put on a parka and a fur coat to paint the living room?
It said on the paint tin, 'For best results, put on two coats.'

Did you hear about the dumb blonde who was found dead from exhaustion in her shower?
The police were baffled until they read the instructions on her shampoo bottle: 'Wet hair. Apply shampoo. Repeat.'

How do you keep a dumb blonde busy for hours?
Put her in a round room and tell her to sit in the corner.

What do you call a dumb blonde hiding in a closet?
The 1987 World Hide and Seek Champion.

How do you sink a submarine full of dumb blondes?
Knock on the door.

What do you call a dumb blonde behind a steering wheel?
An airbag.

What do you do if a dumb blonde throws a grenade at you?
Pull the pin and throw it back.

A hundred dumb blondes are packed into a railway carriage. One of them suddenly calls out, 'Hey, the carriage next door is empty!' So they all get up and go into the next carriage.

A dumb blonde wishes to show off her knowledge of world capitals. 'Go on,' she challenges, 'ask me to name any capital. I know all of them.' 'What's the capital of Spain?' someone asks. 'That's just too easy,' laughs the dumb blonde. 'S.'

Three dumb blondes are determined to prove their intelligence. 'Ask us a question, any question,' they insist to their brunette friend. 'Okay, what's two plus two?' 'Four,' answers the first dumb blonde after a moment's thought. 'Wait!' scream the other two. 'Give her another chance!'

What do smart blondes and UFOs have in common?
You've heard about them but you've never see one.

Why do dumb blondes love lightning?
They think someone is taking their photo.

Did you hear about the dumb blonde who was fired from the banana plantation?
She threw out all the bent ones.

What is a brunette between two dumb blondes?
An interpreter.

What do you call it when a dumb blonde dyes her hair brunette?
Artificial intelligence.

What do dumb blondes and beer bottles have in common?
They are both empty from the neck up.

Two dumb blondes board a bus. The first dumb blonde asks, 'Will this bus take me to London?' The driver shakes his head, 'Sorry, no.' The second dumb blonde smiles, 'Will it take me?'

How did the dumb blonde fish die?
It drowned.

Why are most dumb blonde jokes one-liners?
So men can understand them.

E

Earthquakes

What did the ground say to the earthquake?
'You crack me up!'

What did one earthquake say to the other?
'It's not my fault!'

Why are earthquakes great actors?
They bring the house down.

Why wouldn't the insurance company pay out claims
after the earthquake?
They had a no-fault policy.

See also **Volcanoes**.

Elephants

Why is an elephant large, grey and wrinkled?
Because if it was small, white and smooth it would be an
aspirin.

What's bright red and weighs four tonnes?
An elephant holding its breath.

Why are elephants so wrinkly?
Have you ever tried ironing one?

Why do elephants have big ears?
Because Noddy won't pay the ransom.

Why do elephants have trunks?
Because they'd look ridiculous in bikinis.

What is big and green and has a trunk?
An unripe elephant.

Why couldn't the two elephants go swimming?
They only had one pair of trunks.

Why was the baby elephant worried when his trunk
reached eleven inches in length?
He was afraid it would grow into a foot.

What did the elephant say when the crocodile bit off its
trunk?
'I thuppothe you think thad's fuddy.'

Why are elephants clever?
They have a lot of grey matter.

Why do elephants never forget?
Because nobody ever tells them anything.

What do you call an elephant that is always mumbling?
A mumbo-jumbo.

What time is it when an elephant sits on the fence?
Time to get a new fence.

What do you get if an elephant sits on your best friend?
A flat mate.

How can you tell if there's an elephant in the fridge?
From the footprints in the jelly.

How do you know when an elephant has been sleeping in your bed?
From the peanut crumbs on the pillow.

How do you know when an elephant is hiding under your bed?
From your nose pressing against the ceiling.

How do you lift an elephant?
Place it on an acorn and wait twenty years.

How does an elephant get down from a tree?
He sits on a leaf and waits for autumn.

What is the difference between African elephants and Indian elephants?
About three thousand miles.

Why do elephants paint their feet yellow?
So they can hide upside down in the custard.
(Have you ever seen an elephant hiding upside down in the custard? No? It must work, then.)

Why do elephants paint their toenails red?
To hide in strawberry jam.

What's the red stuff between an elephant's toes?
Slow pygmies.

What's the difference between an elephant and a piece of tissue?
You can't wipe your bottom with an elephant.

Why don't elephants play cards in the jungle?
Because of all the cheetahs.

What did Tarzan say when he saw the elephants coming
on a Tuesday?
'Here come the elephants.'
What did Tarzan say when he saw the elephants coming
on a Tuesday wearing sunglasses?
Nothing. He didn't recognize them.

What is the easiest way to get a wild elephant?
Buy a tame one and annoy it.

How do you get an elephant into a matchbox?
Take the matches out first.

Why did the elephant cross the road?
It was the chicken's day off.

Two elephants fell off a cliff. Boom, boom!

What do you find in an elephants' graveyard?
Elephantoms.

What do you get if you cross an elephant with a mouse?
Great big holes in the skirting board.

What do you get if you cross an elephant with a carpet?
A deep pile in your living room.

What do you get if you cross an elephant with peanut
butter?
An elephant that sticks to the roof of your mouth.

Elves and goblins

What do elves learn at school?
The elfabet.

What do elves do after school?
Gnomework.

Did you hear about the goblin who injured his ankle?
He was a hoblin goblin.

Where do fairies and goblins go when they're feeling ill?
The national elf service.

See also **Gnomes**.

Eskimos

What is an ig?
An Eskimo's house with no loo.

What do Eskimos get if they sit on the ice too long?
Polaroids.

How do Eskimos stop their mouths freezing up?
They grit their teeth.

What do Eskimos buy things with?
Iced lolly.

Two Eskimos sitting in a kayak were chilly, so they lit a
fire in the craft. It sank, proving that you can't have your
kayak and heat it too.

Etiquette See **Manners**.

Examinations

What's black and white and hard all over?
An exam paper.

Teacher I hope I didn't see you cheating just then!
Pupil I hope you didn't as well.

Pupil Please, miss, I don't think I deserve zero for that exam.
Teacher Nor do I, but it's the lowest mark I can give you.

Pupil Mum, you know how you've always been worried about me failing my exams?
Mum Yes?
Pupil Well, your worries are over . . .

'My brother's exam results are underwater.'
'What do you mean?'
'They were all below C level.'

What do you have to take to become a coroner?
A stiff exam.

What kind of tests do they give in witch school?
Hexaminations!

'I was thrown out of college for cheating on the metaphysics exam; I looked into the soul of the boy next to me.' *(Woody Allen)*

See also **School**.

Executions

What did the hangman say to the condemned man?
'Your neck's on my list.'

A lawyer visits a condemned man awaiting the electric chair. 'I've got good news and bad news,' he tells him. 'What's the bad news?' asks the condemned man. 'They won't grant a stay of execution.' 'And the good news?' 'I managed to get your voltage reduced.'

A condemned murderer is placed in the electric chair for execution. When all is ready the prison chaplain approaches the prisoner. 'Have you any last request?' he asks. 'Yes,' replies the prisoner, 'will you hold my hand?'

A condemned man gets a bad case of the hiccups as he is being strapped into the electric chair. 'Any last requests?' asks the warden. 'Yes,' says the prisoner, 'could you, hic, do something to scare me?'

Why did the executioner ask for pen and paper?
So he could write his chopping list.

Exercise

'You have to stay in shape. My grandmother, she started walking five miles a day when she was sixty. She's ninety-seven today and we don't know where the hell she is.'
(Ellen Degeneres)

Did you hear about the man who took up jogging after his doctor said it would add ten years to his life?
Now he feels ten years older.

Why did the forgetful elephant take up running?
To jog his memory.

How can you gain weight through exercise?
Jog backwards.

'Jogging is for people who aren't intelligent enough to watch breakfast TV.' *(Victoria Wood)*

'So I rang up a local building firm. I said, "I want a skip outside my house." He said, "I'm not stopping you." ' *(Tim Vine)*

Why did the aerobics instructor cross the road?
Someone on the other side could still walk.

How do ghost-hunters keep fit?
They exorcize.

'I'm Jewish and I don't work out. If God wanted us to bend over he'd put diamonds on the floor.' *(Joan Rivers)*

See also **Health**.

Extreme sports

If at first you don't succeed, give up skydiving.

Why don't blind people like to skydive?
Because it scares the dog.

What's the difference between a bad golfer and a bad skydiver?
A bad golfer goes 'whack, damn'. A bad skydiver goes 'damn, whack'.

What do you call it when your parachute does not open?
Jumping to a conclusion.

For sale: Parachute, only used once, never opened, small
stain.

F

Families

'Apparently, one in five people in the world are Chinese. And there are five people in my family, so it must be one of them. It's either my mum or my dad. Or my older brother, Colin. Or my younger brother, Ho-Chan-Chu. But I think it's Colin.' *(Tim Vine)*

'Why is your sister so short?'
'She's my half-sister.'

Why are aunties like a box of chocolates?
Some are sweet but you also get nutty ones.

What do aunties take for sore throats?
Auntiseptic.

An old lady is invited to a big family party. 'Honestly, youth today!' she comments as she watches some teenagers dancing. 'That short-haired girl over there in a man's shirt and jeans – you wouldn't know she was a girl at all!' A stranger next to her frowns. 'I think I would – she's my daughter.' 'I'm so sorry,' says the old lady, embarrassed, 'I didn't know you were her father.' 'I'm not,' the other replies, 'I'm her mother.'

'I was doing some decorating, so I got out my step-ladder; I don't get on with my real ladder.' *(Harry Hill)*

See also **Children**; **Grandparents**; **Parents**.

Fancy dress parties *See* **Parties**.

Farming

Why was the farmer hopping mad?
Because someone had trodden on his corn.

There once was a man from Algiers
Who tried growing corn in his ears.
When the temperature rose,
He leapt to his toes,
Now popping is all that he hears.

Two chicken farmers are walking down the lane. One is carrying a sack and the other asks what's in it. 'Chickens,' the man replies. 'How many?' asks his friend. 'I'll tell you what – if you can guess, I'll give you both of 'em.' The other thinks for a moment: 'Six?'

What do you call an Arab dairy farmer?
A milk sheikh.

What has five fingers and drives a tractor?
A farm hand.

Why was the scarecrow given a prize?
For being outstanding in his field.

What do you get if you cross a farmer with an astronaut?
A ploughman's launch.

I had a ploughman's lunch yesterday. He wasn't half cross about it.

See also **Chickens**; **Cows**; **Fruit**; **Pigs**; **Sheep**; **Vegetables**.

Farting See **Manners**.

Fast food

What are the best things you can put in a pizza?
Teeth.

Good King Wenceslas orders a pizza. 'How would you like it?' the waiter asks. 'Same as usual, please: deep pan, crisp and even.'

What's 50 metres tall, crispy round the edges, covered in cheese and tomato and looks like it's about to fall over?
The Leaning Tower of Pizza.

Why are hamburgers better than hot dogs?
Because hot dogs are wurst.

Why didn't the hot dog become a movie star?
The rolls weren't big enough.

Where do burgers sleep?
On beds of lettuce.

See also **Food**.

Fish

Two fish in a tank. One turns to the other and says, 'Do you know how to drive this thing?'

Which fish is the fastest?
The motor pike.

What sort of fish might you find in a birdcage?
A perch.

What do you call a dangerous fish who drinks too much?
A beer-a-cuda.

What kind of fish goes well with ice cream?
Jellyfish.

Why are fish smarter than mice?
Because they live in schools.

How do fish go to school?
By octobus.

Why shouldn't piranhas be allowed in class?
Because they attack in schools.

Where do little fish go when their parents are at work?
Plaice school.

What did the boy fish say to his girlfriend?
'Your plaice or mine?'

Why are fish bad at tennis?
They hate going up to the net.

To whom do fish go to borrow money?
The loan shark.

Where do fish keep their savings?
In offshore accounts.

What is the richest fish in the world?
A goldfish.

Why do fish get such big phone bills?
Because once they're on it they can never get off the line.

What did the fish say when he swam into the concrete wall?
'Dam!'

Why did the fish take an aspirin?
It had a haddock.

What sort of fish can perform surgical operations?
A sturgeon.

Where do fish wash?
In river basins.

Where do fish sleep?
In river beds.

Why did the salmon cross the road?
Just for the halibut.

How far can an Egyptian fish swim?
A Nile and a half.

What do deaf fish wear?
Herring aids.

What kind of fish can't swim?
Dead ones.

Why isn't there any room for customers in the fish and chip shop?
Because the fish fillet.

A man walks into a fishmonger's. 'Do you make fishcakes?' asks the man. 'Sure,' answers the fishmonger. 'Great,' says the man, 'it's his birthday.'

What is the best fish on ice?
A skate.

What do you get if you cross a trout with an apartment?
A flat fish.

What do you get if you cross an elephant with a fish?
Swimming trunks.

See also **Fishing**.

Fishing

What is the difference between a hunter and a fisherman?
A hunter lies in wait and a fisherman waits and lies.

How can you tell when a fisherman is lying?
His mouth is moving.

There are two kinds of fishermen. Those who fish for sport, and those who actually catch something.

There are two times when fishing is fun: before you get there and after you leave.

Give a man a fish and he eats for a day. Teach a man to fish and you get rid of him for the whole weekend.

There was a young fellow named Fisher
Who was fishing for fish in a fissure,
When a trout, with a grin,
Pulled the fisherman in:
Now they're fishing the fissure for Fisher.

Tom, Dick and Harry are out fishing. Suddenly, Tom hooks a huge fish and is pulled right out of the boat and under the water. Dick dives in to rescue his friend and eventually comes back up with Tom in his grasp. As Harry performs mouth-to-mouth resuscitation on Tom, he wrinkles his nose and comments, 'I don't remember Tom having such bad breath!' Dick looks at Tom and says, 'I don't recall Tom wearing a dinner jacket either.'

What kind of money do fishermen make?
Net profits.

A local doctor is well known for catching large fish. While out on a fishing trip he suddenly gets a call summoning him to the bedside of a woman in labour at a farm nearby. He rushes to her aid, delivers the baby and then looks for something to weigh the child with. Having nothing better, he eventually weighs it in his fishing scale. The baby weighs 26 lbs 8 oz.

What do anglers do in radioactive waters?
Nuclear fission.

Two fishermen rent a boat to go fishing in a local lake. By the end of the day they are delighted to find they have caught no less than fifty fish. The first fisherman turns to his friend and says, 'Mark this spot so we know where to come to tomorrow!' The second fisherman finds his penknife and carves a big cross on the side of the boat. 'You idiot!' says the first fisherman. 'What if we don't get the same boat tomorrow?'

How do you catch a school of fish?
With a bookworm.

A father and son go out fishing in a small boat. Unfortunately, as they are getting ready to cast their first lines, the father accidentally drops his wallet into the water. As it sinks, however, a carp swims up and latches onto a corner of it. A moment later a second carp seizes the opposite corner and the fish begin a tussle for possession of the mysterious article. The boy watches with fascination. It is the first time he has seen carp to carp walleting.

See also **Fish**; *Hunting*.

Fleas

Two fleas are coming home from the cinema when it starts to rain. 'Shall we walk?' says the first flea. 'No,' says the second, 'let's take a dog.'

How do fleas go from dog to dog?
They itch a lift.

Two fleas meet in Robinson Crusoe's beard. As one hops off he calls to the other, 'Bye, see you on Friday!'

A flea and a fly in a flue
Were trapped, so they thought, 'What to do?'
'Let us fly,' said the flea,
'Let us flee,' said the fly,
So they flew through a flaw in the flue.

What do you call a cold flea?
Fleazing.

What do fleas wear?
Jump suits.

Why was the mother flea so sad?
Her children all went to the dogs.

How do you set up a flea circus?
From scratch.

How do you start a flea race?
'One, two, flea, go!'

Why did the flea fail his exams?
He didn't come up to scratch.

What did the romantic flea say?
'I love you aw-flea.'

What is the difference between a coyote and a flea?
One howls on the prairie, while the other prowls on the
hairy.

What do you get if you cross a flea with a rabbit?
Bugs Bunny.

Flies

Why did the fly fly?
Because the spider spied 'er.

Why did the two flies rush along the top of the cereal packet?
Because it said 'Tear along the dotted line.'

What do you call a fly with no wings?
A walk.

What's the difference between a bird and a fly?
A bird can fly but a fly can't bird.

Flowers See *Gardening*.

Flying See *Aviation*.

Food

What's yellow and highly dangerous?
Shark-infested custard.

Why was the custard bad-tempered?
It got upset over a trifle.

What's green and miserable?
Apple grumble.

Why did the jelly wobble?
Because it saw the milkshake.

What kind of meringues can't be thrown away?
Boomeringues.

'So I went down my local ice-cream shop, and said, "I want to buy an ice cream." He said, "Hundreds and thousands?" I said, "We'll start with one." ' *(Tim Vine)*

What pie can fly?
A magpie.

What did the pork chop say to the lamb chop?
'Nice to meat you.'

What do you call little piles of rubbish?
Dumplings.

Why is the desert full of food?
Because of all the sandwiches there.

Two men have been lost in the desert for weeks, and are nearly dead with starvation when they stumble on a tree which, to their great surprise and delight, bears rasher upon rasher of bacon. 'It's a bacon tree,' they shout, 'we're saved!' The first man runs towards the tree, but as he gets close he is suddenly shot down in a hail of bullets. The second man takes cover and calls to his stricken friend: 'Hey! What on earth happened?' The first man waves his friend back. 'Watch out, it isn't a bacon tree at all. It's a ham bush!'

How do Welsh people eat cheese?
Caerphilly.

What cheese is made backwards?
Edam.

What do you call someone else's cheese?
Nacho cheese.

What is the difference between a country bumpkin and a Welsh rarebit?
One is easy to cheat and the other is cheesy to eat.

What did one crisp say to the other crisp?
'Let's go for a dip.'

Did you hear about the fight in the biscuit tin?
The bandit hit the penguin over the head with a club, tied him to a wagon wheel with a blue ribbon and made his breakaway in a taxi.

Which cake lives in a French cathedral?
The flapjack of Notre Dame.

Why did the baker give up making doughnuts?
He was fed up with the hole business.

What do they eat in heaven?
Angel cakes.

What are two things you cannot have for breakfast?
Lunch and dinner.

Did you hear about the man who drowned in a bowl of muesli?
He was dragged in by a strong currant.

What do you get if you cross bread with a bell?
Bunting.

There was a young girl from Berlin
Whose nose was exceedingly thin.
She could slice up the butter
With barely a mutter,
And flip it down onto her chin.

What's the best way to stop food going bad?
Eat it.

'Why do you eat so fast?'
'I don't want to lose my appetite.'

There once was a fat boy called Kidd
Who ate twenty mince pies for a quid.
When asked 'Are you faint?'
He replied, 'No, I ain't,
But I don't feel as well as I did!'

See also **Cooking**; **Drink**; **Fast food**; **Fruit**;
Restaurants; **Vegetables**.

Football

Why didn't the football player want to travel by plane?
He was afraid he would be put on the wing.

What do you get if you drop a piano on a team's defence?
A flat back four.

What did the manager do when the football pitch
flooded?
Sent on the subs.

Why did the football player kick his computer?
To boot up the system.

Why couldn't the car play football?
It only had one boot.

What position did the ghost play on the football team?
Ghoulkeeper.

Why was the tiny ghost invited to join the football team?
They needed a little team spirit.

When do football pitches become triangles?
When someone takes a corner.

Why did the manager give his team lighters?
Because they kept losing their matches.

Did you hear about the goalkeeper who was also a
volunteer fire officer? When a woman and her baby were
trapped in a burning building he shouted at the woman to
throw him the baby: 'I won't drop him – I'm a professional
goalkeeper!' The woman tossed him the baby, which he
caught safely, then bounced three times and kicked over
the garden wall.

What do you call a German footballer who scores three
goals?
A geriatric.

What happened to the football player when his eyesight
started to fail?
He became a referee.

What do you call a girl standing behind the goal on a
football pitch?
Annette.

Why was Cinderella left out of the football team?
She ran away from the ball.

Why was Cinderella no good at football?
Her coach was a pumpkin.

Foreign countries See **Geography**.

Foreign languages

Latin is a language,
As dead as dead can be,
First it killed the Romans,
Now it's killing me.

'In French, oeuf means egg, cheese is fromage . . . it's like those French have a different word for everything.' *(Steve Martin)*

What does a Spanish farmer say to his chickens?
'Olé.'

A Frenchman staying in an English hotel rings reception: 'I'd like some pepper, please.' 'Black or white pepper, sir?' asks the receptionist. 'Neither,' the Frenchman replies, 'toilet pepper!'

A man eating in a Chinese restaurant decides to complain to the waitress about his meal. 'This chicken is rubbery,' he tells her. 'Thank you,' replies the waitress, with a smile.

'I bet I can get you to speak like a native American.'
'How?'

Fortune-tellers See **Psychics**.

Frogs and toads

Where do tadpoles change into frogs?
In the croakroom.

What's green and can jump a mile a minute?
A frog with hiccups.

What do you call a frog with no hind legs?
Unhoppy.

What's green and hard?
A frog with a flick knife.

What goes 'dot, dot, dash, croak, dash, dot, ribbet'?
Morse toad.

Why did the female frog lay no eggs?
Because the male frogs spawned her affections.

Where do frogs keep their savings?
In river banks.

Where do you take a frog with bad eyesight?
A hoptician.

What happens if a frog's car breaks down?
It gets toad away.

How did the sunbathing frog die?
Heat croak.

What do you get if you cross a frog with a dog?
A croaker spaniel.

What do you get if you cross a frog with a chair?
A toadstool.

Fruit

What's blue and square?
An orange in disguise.

Why did the orange go to the doctor?
He wasn't peeling well.

Why did the orange stop rolling down the hill?
It ran out of juice.

What do you call a revolving orange?
A merry-go-rind.

What did the apple say to the orange?
Nothing. Apples don't talk.

'Doctor, doctor, I keep thinking I'm an apple!'
'We must get to the core of this.'

Why did the apple cry?
Its peelings were hurt.

What can a whole apple do that half an apple can't?
Look round.

Why did the apple turnover?
Because it saw the cheese roll.

What's worse than finding a maggot in your apple?
Finding half a maggot in your apple.

Rhubarb: celery with high blood pressure.

Why don't melons run away to get married?
Because they cantaloupe.

How do you tease fruit?
'Banananananana!'

What kind of key do you need to open a banana?
A monkey.

How can you tell the difference between a banana and a hippo?
You can't pick a hippo up.

What's the difference between a banana and an elephant?
You can't peel an elephant.

What do you get if you cross a banana with a clown?
Peels of laughter.

If a crocodile makes shoes, what does a banana make?
Slippers.

'Knock, knock.'
'Who's there?'
'Banana.'
'Banana who?'
'Knock, knock.'
'Who's there?'
'Banana.'
'Banana who?'

'Knock, knock.'
'Who's there?'
'Orange.'
'Orange who?'
'Orange you glad I didn't say banana?'

Why aren't they growing bananas any longer?
They're long enough already.

What's yellow and grows in apple trees?
A stupid banana.

Why do bananas use suntan oil?
Because they peel.

What do you do with a damaged lemon?
Give it lemonaid.

What's blue and shouts for help?
A damson in distress.

Why did the raisin ask the prune to go to the cinema?
Because he couldn't find a date.

What do a grape and an elephant have in common?
They're both purple, except for the elephant.

What did the grape do when the elephant stood on it?
It gave a little wine.

What do you get when two strawberries meet?
A strawberry shake.

What do you get when two strawberries meet at a rock
concert?
A strawberry crush.

What do you get when two strawberries meet at a waxing parlour?
A strawberry smoothie.

What did one strawberry say to the other?
'It's because of you we're in this jam.'

What did one tomato say to the other tomato?
'Go on ahead and I'll ketchup.'

See also **Food**.

Funerals

Always go to other people's funerals, or they won't go to yours.

There once was a fellow named Clyde
Who went to a funeral and cried.
When asked who was dead,
He stammered and said,
'I don't know, I just came for the ride.'

Did you hear about the undertakers who buried the wrong body?
They made a grave error.

Why is it so hard to bury an elephant?
Because it is a huge undertaking.

See also **Death**; **Undertakers**.

G

Gambling

How can you win a small fortune in Las Vegas?
Spend a large fortune.

Did you hear about the gambler who complained that he
seemed to win one day and lose the next?
Now he gambles only every other day.

Did you hear about the gypsy who won the lottery?
He was paid in travellers' cheques.

An old lady wins a million pounds on the lottery. Her
family are afraid the shock of the news will be too much
for her, so they ask the family doctor to break it to her for
them. The doctor goes into her bedroom and after some
routine chat casually asks the old lady, 'Tell me, what
would you do if you won a million pounds?' The old lady
pats him on the knee and smiles, 'Well, you've been so
nice to me, doctor, I would give half of it to you.' The
doctor collapses and dies of shock.

A young man is flat broke so prays to God to let him win
the lottery. That week, however, he has no luck. The
following week he prays again that God might let him win
the lottery. Once again, however, he wins nothing. The
third week he prays to God one last time, threatening to

kill himself if he does not win. This time a voice suddenly booms from the sky above: 'Listen, meet me halfway on this – at least buy a ticket!'

'Knock, knock.'
'Who's there?'
'Bet.'
'Bet who?'
'Bet you don't know who's knocking on your door!'

Gangsters

Which criminal mastermind lives underwater?
The Codfather.

Who is the biggest gangster in the rock pool?
Al Caprawn.

What were the gangster's last words?
'Who put that violin in my violin case!'

How many men do you need for a Mafia funeral?
Just one. To slam the car boot shut.

See also **Criminals**.

Gardening

Why do gardeners plant bulbs?
So the worms can see where they are going.

Did you hear about the successful bonsai gardener?
He's looking for a house with a smaller garden.

A small boy sees a gardener pushing a wheelbarrow full of manure. 'What are you going to do with that?' he asks. 'Put it on my strawberries,' says the gardener. 'Yuk!' says the small boy. 'We have cream on ours.'

An indolent vicar of Bray
His roses allowed to decay;
His wife, more alert,
Bought a powerful squirt,
And said to her spouse, 'Let us spray.'

There was a young man from Leeds
Who swallowed a packet of seeds;
Within just one hour
His nose was a flower
And his head was a riot of weeds.

What runs round a garden but never moves?
A fence.

A gardener, living in Ewell,
Found his bonfire wanted more fuel;
So they threw Uncle James
To heighten the flames –
A measure effective though cruel.

What kind of flower grows on your face?
Tulips.

'My neighbour asked if he could use my lawnmower and I told him of course he could, so long as he didn't take it out of my garden.' *(Eric Morecambe)*

Old gardeners never die, they just go to pot.

See also **Trees**.

Genies

A man releases a genie from a bottle and is granted three wishes. 'What I'd like,' he announces after a moment's thought, 'is a bottle of beer that will never be empty.' There is a flash and a bottle of beer appears in his hand. He drinks from it and finds, to his delight, that it remains just as full after he has drunk as it was when he started. 'What would you like for your other wishes?' asks the genie. The man grins. 'I'll have two more of these!'

A man releases a genie from a bottle and is granted three wishes. After his first two wishes come true he cannot think of a third and so takes the bottle round to his best friend, so that he can have the last wish. After being told about the genie, the friend thinks for a moment and then says, 'I'd like a million bucks, please.' Immediately, the whole house is filled with ducks. 'I forgot to say,' responds the first man, 'he's a little deaf.'

A man releases a genie from a bottle and is granted three wishes. 'I'd like a million pounds, please,' says the man for his first wish, and immediately a million pounds land at his feet. 'I'd like a new car,' he then wishes, and a top-of-the-range sports car materializes before him. The man thinks long and hard about his final wish and finally decides, 'I'd like to be irresistible to women.' There is a dazzling flash – and he is transformed into a box of chocolates.

A prawn called Bob frees a genie from a bottle and is granted two wishes. Bob decides that he would like to become a shark and is instantly transformed. He soon finds out, however, that all his old friends are now afraid of him so he uses his second wish to become a prawn once again. Bob then swims off to his mate Christian's house and knocks on the door. 'Go away,' says Christian, 'I'm scared you'll eat me!' 'No, I won't,' Bob shouts back, 'I'm a prawn again Christian.'

Two brunettes and a dumb blonde are lost in the desert, when they find a genie lamp. Once released, the genie says he will grant them one wish each. The first brunette wishes to go home and is whisked away. The second brunette says she would like to be in a luxury hotel with her boyfriend, and is similarly dispatched. Finally, it's the dumb blonde's turn. She thinks for a moment and then tells the genie she's lonely and wants the other two back.

Geography

What do you need to be good at geography?
Abroad knowledge of the subject.

What is the biggest rope in the world?
Europe.

'Knock, knock.'
'Who's there?'
'Europe.'
'Europe who?'
'Europe early this morning!'

Why is Europe like a frying pan?
Because it has Greece at the bottom.

'Knock, knock.'
'Who's there?'
'Francis.'
'Francis who?'
'Francis a country in Europe.'

Teacher What is the capital of France?
Pupil F.

Which French tourist attraction is made of jelly, cream, custard, sponge and fruit?
The Trifle Tower.

'I'm glad I wasn't born in France.'
'Why?'
'I'm not French.'

Teacher If a person from Rome is called a Roman, what is a person from Paris called?
Pupil A parasite?

Teacher What do we get from Germany?
Pupil Germs?

What is the coldest place on Earth?
Chile.

Where are the Andes?
At the end of your armies.

What kind of cans do you get in Mexico?
Mexicans.

'Where is your mother from?'
'Alaska.'
'It's all right, I'll ask her myself.'

Teacher Lucy, which is farther away – America or the moon?
Lucy America. You can see the moon, but you can't see America.

Why does the Mississippi wander about so much?
Even though it has four eyes it can't see where it's going.

'Where do you come from?'
'Scotland.'
'Which part?'
'All of me.'

Why does Mount Everest have such good hearing?
It has so many mountain ears.

See also **Earthquakes**; **Volcanoes**.

Ghosts

Why didn't the ghost go to the ball?
He had no body to go with.

Who did the ghost take to the dance?
His ghoulfriend.

What did the mummy ghost say to the naughty baby ghost?
'Spook when you're spooken to.'

What do ghosts eat for breakfast?
Dreaded wheat.

What do ghosts eat for lunch?
Spooketti.

What do ghosts eat for dinner?
Ghoulash.

What do ghosts have for dessert?
Ice scream.

Where do ghosts live?
In dead ends.

Where do Australian ghosts live?
The Northern Terrortory.

What game do ghosts like to play?
Hide and shriek.

Which is the ghost's favourite ride at the funfair?
The rollerghoster.

How do ghosts get through locked doors?
They use skeleton keys.

Why did the ghost see an astrologer?
He wanted to know his horrorscope.

How do you get a ghost to lie perfectly flat?
Use a spirit level.

What do you call a drunken ghost?
A methylated spirit.

What do short-sighted ghosts wear?
Spooktacles.

What trees do ghouls like best?
Cemetrees.

How can you make a ghost-proof bicycle?
Remove the spooks.

What do you call a prehistoric ghost?
A terrordactyl.

What do you call a haunted chicken?
A poultrygeist.

How do ghosts start their letters?
'Tomb it may concern . . .'

Why was the ghost arrested?
He didn't have a haunting licence.

Why are cemeteries such noisy places?
Because of all the coffin.

What does a headless horseman ride?
A nightmare.

Why do demons get on so well with ghouls?
Because demons are a ghoul's best friend.

What is a devils' picket line called?
A demonstration.

Did you hear about the man who forgot to pay his
exorcist?
He was repossessed.

What do you get if you try to take photographs of a ghost?
Transparencies.

What is the best day of the week for seeing ghosts?
Frightday.

What do you get if you cross a ghost with an Italian landmark?
The screaming tower of Pisa.

What do you get if you cross a ghost with Bambi?
Bamboo.

See also **Skeletons**.

Giraffes

Why do giraffes have such long necks?
Because their heads are so far away from their bodies.

Seriously, why do giraffes have such long necks?
Their feet smell.

Why are giraffes brave?
Because they stick their necks out.

Why do giraffes take so long to say sorry?
It takes them ages to swallow their pride.

Where are giraffes educated?
In high school.

What's worse than a giraffe with a sore throat?
A centipede with athlete's foot.

What do you get if you cross a giraffe with a porcupine?
A walking toilet brush.

What do you get if you cross a giraffe with a hedgehog?
A long-necked toothbrush.

Glow-worms

Why was the glow-worm unhappy?
Because her children weren't very bright.

What do glow-worms eat?
Light meals.

What do you get if you put a glow-worm in water?
A floodlight.

What do you get if you cross a glow-worm with a glass of beer?
Light ale.

Gnomes

Where do gnomes go at night?
Gnome sweet gnome.

Why are gnomes so fat?
They can't stop goblin.

Which government department is responsible for gnome affairs?
The Gnome Office.

Where do gnomes live?
Gnome Man's Land.

*See also **Elves and goblins**.*

Goats

'Knock, knock.'
'Who's there?'
'Goat.'
'Goat who?'
'Goat to the door and find out!'

'Doctor, doctor, I keep thinking I'm a goat!'
'How long have you felt like this?'
'Since I was a kid.'

What is another name for a mountain goat?
A hillbilly.

What do you get if you cross a goat with a cow and a sheep?
The Milky Baa Kid.

Golf

'I just played golf for the first time.'
'How did you get on?'
'It took me seventy-one strokes.'
'That's brilliant!'
'Yes, tomorrow I'm going on to the second hole.'

First golfer How should I have played that last shot?
Second golfer Under an assumed name.

A hopeless golfer asks a professional for tips. After watching him play, the professional observes drily, 'You're standing too close to the ball . . . after you've hit it.'

A golfer who sought to survive
With grit, dedication and drive,
'Inflation,' he'd claim,
'Is affecting my game,
I used to shout "fore" – now it's "five"!'

A golfer turns to his caddy as they leave the last hole. 'Do you think my game's improving?' he asks. The caddy nods. 'Certainly. You miss the ball much closer than you used to.'

Two men are playing a round of golf when a funeral cortège passes by. One of the men doffs his cap and stands in silence until it has gone. 'Not often you see people showing respect like that these days,' the other player observes. 'Well,' says the other man, replacing his cap, 'I felt I should. After all, we were married for twenty-seven years.'

A golfer gets very excited about his new golf ball. He explains to his friends that it is impossible to lose: if the ball goes into the long grass it will light up, if it goes into the water it will release a flag to mark its position and in failing light it will produce a high-pitched beeping noise so that it can be easily located. 'Where on earth did you get it?' his friends demand. 'I found it.'

A vicar and a lawyer are playing golf. The lawyer is not having a good day. When he misses an easy putt he groans, 'Damn! Missed!' A few minutes later the lawyer makes another mistake, upon which he mutters, 'Damn! Missed again!' In fact, every time he plays a bad shot he fumes, 'Damn! Missed!' After a dozen holes the vicar finally loses patience. 'If you do not stop using such language, sir, the Lord will strike you down!' Just then there is a dazzling flash and the vicar is fried to a crisp by a bolt of lightning. As the smoke clears a deep voice is heard rumbling overhead, 'Damn! Missed!'

'Knock, knock.'
'Who's there?'
'Adolf.'
'Adolf who?'
'A dolf ball hid me in der moud and now I can't dalk proper.'

What do you get if you cross a golfer with a maths teacher?
A teetotaller.

'Give me my golf clubs, fresh air and a beautiful partner, and you keep my golf clubs and the fresh air.' *(Jack Benny)*

Gorillas

What do you call a gorilla in headphones?
Anything you like. He can't hear you.

Why do gorillas have big nostrils?
Because they have big fingers.

What is gorilla warfare?
Two apes in a fight over a banana.

How do you catch a gorilla?
Hide in a tree and make a noise like a banana.

What do you get if you cross a cat with a gorilla?
An animal that puts you out at night.

See also **Monkeys**.

Grandparents

'Knock, knock.'
'Who's there?'
'Nana.'
'Nana who?'
'Nana your business.'

What is small, pink, wrinkly and belongs to Grandpa?
Grandma.

My granddad is so wrinkly he has to screw his hat on.

Did you hear about the granny who plugged her electric
blanket into the toaster?
She spent the night popping out of bed.

'My grandmother took a bath every year, whether she was
dirty or not.' *(Brendan Behan)*

'Knock, knock.'
'Who's there?'
'Granny.'
'Granny who?'
'Knock, knock.'
'Who's there?'
'Granny.'
'Granny who?'
'Knock, knock.'
'Who's there?'
'Granny.'
'Granny who?'
'Knock, knock.'
'Who's there?'

'Aunt.'
'Aunt who?'
'Aren't you glad Granny's gone?'

See also **Families**.

H

Hair

'I want a hair cut, please.'
'Certainly, which one?'

What do you call a hairdresser's licence?
A permit.

How does the man in the moon cut his hair?
Eclipse it.

Why do hairdressers make good taxi drivers?
Because they know all the shortcuts.

Did you hear about the woman who tried that new
revitalizing shampoo?
Her hair was awake all night.

There was an old man from Whitehaven
Whose whiskers had never been shaven.
He said, 'It is best,
For they make a nice nest,
In which I can keep my pet raven!'

What do you get if you cross a ghost with a barber?
A scaredresser.

See also **Baldness**.

Hares See **Rabbits**.

Health

'Health is what my friends are always drinking to before they fall down.' *(Phyllis Diller)*

How do you prevent a summer cold?
Catch it in the winter.

What happens if you eat yeast and shoe polish?
Every morning you'll rise and shine.

A young woman falls into conversation with a wrinkled old man in the park and asks him what is his secret for a long, happy life. 'I smoke a packet of cigarettes every day,' the old man explains, 'I drink a bottle of vodka every weekend, I eat only fast food and I never exercise.' 'But that's incredible!' says the woman. 'Do you mind me asking what age you are?' 'Of course not,' says the man. 'I'm twenty-seven.'

See also **Diets**; **Exercise**; **Ill-health**.

Higher education

A maiden at college, Miss Breeze,
Weighed down by BAs and LitDs
Collapsed from the strain.
Said her doctor, 'It's plain –
You're killing yourself by degrees.'

A professor is someone who talks in someone else's sleep.

How do you become a professor?
By degrees.

'People knock Asbos, but you have to bear in mind they're the only qualification some of these kids are ever going to get.' *(Linda Smith)*

See also **School**.

Hippies

Where does one find hippies?
At the top of one's leggies.

What was the hippy's wife called?
Mississippi.

Why didn't the lifeguard save the hippy?
Because he was too far out, man.

How do you get a hippy out of the bath?
Turn on the water.

History

Why is history like a fruit cake?
Because it is full of dates.

Why was the archaeologist upset?
His job was in ruins.

Teacher We had the Ice Age and then the Stone Age – what came next?
Pupil The sausage?

Which ruler of Ancient Egypt did the washing-up?
Pharaoh Liquid.

What was the speed limit in ancient Egypt?
Sixty Niles per hour.

Why were the pyramids of ancient Egypt fitted with car horns?
So you could toot 'n' come in.

What do Alexander the Great and Winnie-the-Pooh have in common?
Their second name.

Why do we know that Rome was built at night?
Because it wasn't built in a day.

How did Hannibal become the first geneticist?
He crossed the Alps with elephants.

How was the Roman Empire divided?
With a pair of Caesars.

Julius Caesar orders Brutus to get him a dozen apples. Brutus soon returns and hands the apples to Caesar. On counting them, Caesar finds only ten. Angrily, he turns to Brutus and snarls, 'Et tu, Brute?'

What was Camelot famous for?
Its knightlife.

Who made the Round Table for King Arthur?
Sir Cumference.

Why were the centuries before the Norman Conquest
called the Dark Ages?
Because there were so many knights.

Who was round and shiny and invaded England?
William the Conker.

Where did King John sign the Magna Carta?
At the bottom.

Who invented the fountain pen?
The Incas.

Why did Henry VIII have so many wives?
He liked to chop and change.

Why did Henry VIII have skittles on his lawn?
So he could take Anne Boleyn.

Teacher Can anyone tell me in which battle Lord Nelson
was killed?
Pupil His last one.

An American tourist is being shown a raised brass plaque
on the deck of HMS *Victory*, marking where Nelson was
mortally wounded. 'That's where Nelson fell,' the guide
announces solemnly. 'I'm not surprised,' responds the
American, 'I nearly tripped over it myself.'

Where did Napoleon keep his armies?
Up his sleevies.

What did they call the emperor of France after he was hit by a cannonball?
Napoleon Blownapart.

'One of my ancestors was killed at Waterloo.'
'Which platform?'

Who was the first English monarch to have a mobile phone?
William of Orange.

'I wish I had lived in the olden days.'
'Why?'
'There wasn't so much history to learn then.'

'I thought of becoming a history teacher, but there's no future in it.'

Holidays

What is the best day to go to the beach?
Sunday.

'I just took the wife to the West Indies.'
'Jamaica?'
'No, she came of her own accord.'

'I'm taking the wife to northern Italy this year.'
'Genoa?'
'I should think so, we've been married for twenty years.'

'My wife's gone on holiday to St Petersburg.'
'Is she Russian?'
'No, she's taking her time.'

What's grey and has a trunk?
A mouse going on holiday.
What's brown and has a trunk?
The mouse coming home again.

What's brown and hairy, wears sunglasses and carries a
suitcase?
A coconut going on holiday.

Why is a guidebook like a pair of handcuffs?
Because it is for tourists (two wrists).

What do demons have on holiday?
A devil of a time.

Where do ghosts go on holiday?
The Dead Sea.

See also **Travel**.

Homework

Pupil Miss, should someone be punished for something
they have not done?
Teacher No, certainly not.
Pupil Oh, good, because I haven't done my homework.

A small boy asks his father to help him with his
homework. 'Now, son,' says his father sternly, 'that
wouldn't be right, would it?' 'I suppose not,' says the boy,
'but have a try anyway.'

Teacher Did your mother help you with your homework?
Pupil No, miss. She did it all.

Teacher This homework looks like it was written by your dad.
Pupil Well, I borrowed his pen.

Teacher Where is your homework on time travel?
Pupil I promise I'll hand it in yesterday.

What do Chinese schoolchildren do at home?
Homewok.

Horses

Why does a horse have six legs?
Because it has forelegs in front and two behind.

How do horses propose?
They go down on bended neigh.

When does a cart come before a horse?
In a dictionary.

What kind of horse can swim underwater?
A seahorse.

What sport do horses like best?
Stable tennis.

Why can't horses dance?
They have two left feet.

A horse walks into a bar. The barman says, 'Why the long face?'

What's the difference between a sick horse and a dead bee?
One is a seedy beast and the other is a bee deceased.

Where do they treat sick horses?
Horsepital.

What do you give a pony with a cold?
Cough stirrup.

What did the pony say when he coughed?
'Sorry, I'm just a little horse.'

What is the slowest horse in the world?
A clotheshorse.

Three racehorses are discussing their recent form. The first
horse boasts, 'Of my last fifteen races, I've won eight.' The
second horse replies, 'Well, I've won nineteen of my last
twenty-seven races.' 'That's pretty good,' says the third
horse, 'but of my last thirty-six races, I've won twenty-
eight.' At this point a greyhound dog, who has been
sitting near by and listening, joins in: 'I don't like to boast,
but of my last ninety races, I've won eighty-eight!' The
horses gasp in amazement. 'Wow!' says one, after a
hushed silence. 'A talking dog!'

Hospitals

'Were you long in the hospital?'
'No, I was the same size that I am now.'

Did you hear about the man who was thrown out of the
hospital?
He took a turn for the nurse.

What do you get if you add thirteen hospital patients to
thirteen hospital patients?
Twenty sicks.

What kind of ghosts haunt hospitals?
Surgical spirits.

*See also **Doctor**, **doctor**; **Doctors**; **Ill-health**.*

Houses

What kind of house weighs the least?
A lighthouse.

What does a house wear?
Address.

Why did the house go to the doctor?
It had window pane.

What room has no walls, floor, ceiling or windows?
A mushroom.

What did one wall say to the other wall?
'I'll meet you at the corner.'

What did one lift say to the other?
'I think I'm coming down with something.'

What do you call a pair of housecleaners?
Partners in grime.

*See also **Housework**.*

Housework

Did you hear about the world's laziest housekeeper?
She swept the room with a glance.

'You make the beds, you do the dishes, and six months later you have to start all over again.' *(Joan Rivers)*

'I'm an excellent housekeeper. Every time I get a divorce, I keep the house.' *(Zsa Zsa Gabor)*

A door-to-door salesperson offers a housewife a can of furniture polish: 'It's so good it will do half your work for you.' The woman shrieks with delight: 'In that case I'll take two cans!'

Hunting

Two men are out bear hunting when they find themselves without their weapons and confronted by an angry grizzly. As the bear approaches, snarling, one of the men quickly whips off his boots and pulls on a pair of trainers. 'What are you doing?' asks the other. 'You'll never outrun a grizzly!' 'I don't have to,' replies the the first man, 'I only have to outrun you!'

How do you kill a blue elephant?
With a blue shotgun.
How do you kill a pink elephant?
Twist his trunk until he turns blue and then use a blue shotgun.

There was a young hunter named Shepherd
Who was eaten for lunch by a leopard.
Said the leopard, 'Egad!
You'd be tastier, lad,
If you had only been salted and peppered.'

What do you call a boomerang that doesn't work?
A stick.

'I once shot an elephant in my pyjamas. How he got into my pyjamas, I'll never know.' *(Groucho Marx)*

See also **Fishing**.

Husbands and wives

My husband and I married for better or worse. He couldn't do better and I couldn't do worse.

'I was cleaning out the attic the other day with the wife. Filthy, dirty and covered with cobwebs . . . but she's good with the kids.' *(Tommy Cooper)*

Husband I'm going to make you the happiest woman in the world.
Wife I'll miss you.

Did you hear about the actor who got to play a man who's been married for twenty years?
Next time he hopes to get a speaking part.

Two men are discussing what their wives think of them. The first man says, 'My wife thinks so much of me that she won't let me do any work around the house.' The second man says, 'That's nothing. My wife thinks I'm God.' 'She thinks you're God?' replies the first man. 'What makes you say that?' 'It's obvious. Every night she places a burned offering before me.'

'Husbands are like fires. They go out when unattended.'
(Zsa Zsa Gabor)

Husband Put your coat on. I'm going to the pub.
Wife How nice! Are you taking me out?
Husband No, I'm turning the heating off.

'I was with my wife and she was reading a magazine and
she showed me a photograph of a fur coat. She said, "I'd
like that." So I cut it out and gave it to her.' *(Tommy
Cooper)*

Police officer I'm sorry to be the bearer of sad tidings, but
your wife just fell down the wishing well.
Husband It works!

'Basically, my wife was immature. I'd be at home in the
bath and she'd come in whenever she felt like it and sink
my boats.' *(Woody Allen)*

A police officer flags down an elderly driver and says,
'Excuse me, sir, didn't you realize your wife fell out of your
car three miles back?' 'Thank God,' the old man replies,
'I thought I'd gone deaf!'

Lady Astor If you were my husband I'd poison your
brandy.
Winston Churchill If you were my wife I'd drink it.

A woman is showing off a huge diamond on her finger to
some new friends. 'This is the Klopman diamond, worth
millions,' she tells them, 'but there's a terrible curse that
goes with it.' 'What is it?' ask her friends breathlessly. 'Mr
Klopman.'

Knowing he is about to die, a millionaire changes his will. His wife, with whom he has never got on, will get everything on condition that she remarries within three months of her husband's death. When asked why he is doing this the millionaire explains, 'Because I want someone to be sorry I died.'

A married woman goes into a gunshop and says she's looking for a gun for her husband. 'What gauge did he ask for?' the gunsmith inquires. 'I haven't told him about it,' the woman replies patiently. 'He doesn't even know I'm going to shoot him.'

It's not true that married men live longer than single men. It only seems longer.

There are two entrances to heaven. Over one hangs a sign saying 'Henpecked Husbands'. There is an extremely long line in front of that entrance. Over the other entrance hangs a sign saying 'He-men'. There is just one little old man waiting at that entrance. St Peter notices him and asks him why he is waiting there. The little old man shrugs apologetically. 'My wife told me to stand here.'

*See also **Marriage**; **Men**; **Women**.*

I

Idiots

'What do you mean by going round telling everyone I'm an idiot?'
'Sorry, I didn't know it was a secret.'

'Have you heard about the idiot who keeps saying "no"?'
'No.'
'Oh, so it's you.'

Why do idiots eat biscuits?
Because they're crackers.

Did you hear about the idiot who had a brain transplant?
The brain rejected him.

Did you hear about the idiot who painted his sundial with luminous paint?
He wanted to be able to tell the time at night.

Why did the idiot jump up and down?
He'd taken his medicine but forgotten to shake the bottle.

How do you confuse an idiot?
Forty-two.

How do you keep an idiot in suspense?
I'll tell you tomorrow.

*See also **Dumb blondes**; **Stupidity**.*

Ignorance *See **Stupidity**.*

Ill-health

A man goes to see the doctor. He has a carrot in his right ear, a banana in his left ear and a cucumber up his nose. 'What's the matter with me?' he asks the doctor. The doctor replies, 'You're not eating properly.'

What should you look for if you are about to throw up in church?
The sick box.

'Knock, knock.'
'Who's there?'
'Archie.'
'Archie who?'
'Bless you!'

What are hankies useful for?
Cold storage.

What's stupid and chilly?
A thick cold.

What does a ghost take for a cold?
Coffin drops.

There once was a man named Clegm
Who had a great deal of phlegm.
Ahegm, ahegm,
Ahegm, ahegm,
Ahegm, ahegm, ahegm.

She stood on the bridge at midnight,
Her lips were all a-quiver;
She gave a cough, her leg fell off
And floated down the river.

There's an arthritic lady in Fakenham
Whose joints have a worsening ache in 'em;
Her pain level's rising,
Which isn't surprising:
She's got pills, but hasn't been takin' 'em.

What's grey with red spots?
An elephant with the measles.

What do you give an elephant with an upset stomach?
Plenty of room.

What did one virus say to the other?
'Keep away! I think I've got penicillin!'

What is a terminal illness?
When you are sick at the airport.

'Doctor, doctor, I hope I'm ill!'
'Why do you say that?'
'I'd hate to feel this bad when I'm well!'

What do you call a sick chemist?
Indispensable.

Insanity

Did you hear about the man who jumped off a bridge in Paris?
He went in Seine.

Hello. Let me introduce ourselves.

A young schizophrenic named Struther,
When told of the death of his mother,
Said, 'Yes, it's too bad,
But I can't feel too sad.
After all, I still have each other.'

Did you hear about the paranoid with low self-esteem?
He was afraid no one was out to get him.

'My brother thinks he's a chicken; we don't talk him out of it because we need the eggs.' *(Groucho Marx)*

What do you call a crazy chicken?
A cuckoo cluck.

'My wife's gone mad in Venezuela.'
'Caracas?'
'Yes, absolutely barking.'

What's the definition of a nervous breakdown?
A chameleon on a tartan rug.

A Freudian slip is when you say one thing but mean your mother.

Two inmates of an asylum meet in the corridor. 'I'm Napoleon!' says the first. 'How do you know?' asks the second. 'God told me,' says the first. The second man shakes his head: 'No, I didn't.'

A man visits the psychiatrist wearing a steel helmet, wellington boots and women's underwear. 'Doctor!' he announces. 'I'm worried about my brother.'

'Doctor, doctor, you remember those voices in my head that I've been complaining about for years?'
'Yes, I remember.'
'They've gone!'
'Great. So what's the problem?'
'I think I'm going deaf.'

'Doctor, doctor, I'm a manic depressive.'
'Calm down, cheer up, calm down, cheer up, calm down . . .'

See also **Psychiatrists**.

Insects

What goes 'ninety-nine thud, ninety-nine thud'?
A centipede with a wooden leg.

'Knock, knock.'
'Who's there?'
'Amos.'
'Amos who?'
'Amosquito.'

'Knock, knock.'
'Who's there?'
'Anna.'
'Anna who?'
'Annather mosquito.'

Did you hear about the scientist who tamed a wild mosquito?
Now he has it eating out of his hand.

What has antlers and sucks your blood?
A moosequito.

Have you ever seen a horsefly?
No, but I've seen a chicken run.

What should you do if you are allergic to biting insects?
Avoid biting any.

*See also **Ants**; **Bees**; **Butterflies**; **Fleas**; **Flies**; **Glow-worms**; **Moths***.

Invisibility

The invisible man married the invisible woman. Their children were nothing to look at.

What is red and invisible?
No tomatoes.

How do frogs turn invisible?
They use croaking devices.

'Do you have any invisible ink?'
'Certainly, sir. What colour?'

'Doctor, doctor, I keep thinking I am invisible!'
'Who said that?'

J

Judges

'I could have been a judge but I never had the Latin.' *(Peter Cook)*

What do you call a judge with no thumbs?
Just his fingers.

When an ambitious lawyer hears that a well-known judge has just died he quickly telephones his superiors to let them know he would be willing to take his place. Their reply is not slow in coming: 'That's fine with us, but you'd better check with the undertaker.'

Old judges never die, they just cease to try.

*See also **Courts of law**; **Criminals**; **Prison**.*

Kangaroos

When do kangaroos go on holiday?
Spring.

What do angry kangaroos do?
Get hopping mad.

Why did the mother kangaroo throw the baby kangaroo out?
For smoking in bed.

What do you call an exhausted kangaroo?
Out of bounds.

What do you get if you cross a kangaroo with a sheep?
A woolly jumper.

What do you get if you cross a kangaroo with a mink?
A fur jumper with pockets.

What do you get if you cross a kangaroo with an elephant?
Great big holes all over Australia.

Knock, knock

'Knock, knock.'
'Who's there?'
'Bella.'
'Bella who?'
'Bella not working, that's why I knocka.'

'Knock, knock.'
'Who's there?'
'Boo.'
'Boo who?'
'Don't cry, it's only a joke!'

'Knock, knock.'
'Who's there?'
'Hal.'
'Hal who?'
'Hal who to you too!'

'Knock, knock.'
'Who's there?'
'Heaven.'
'Heaven who?'
'Heaven you heard enough of these silly knock-knock jokes?'

'Knock, knock.'
'Who's there?'
'Howard.'
'Howard who?'
'Howard you like to stand out here in the cold while some idiot keeps asking, "Who's there?"'

'Knock, knock.'
'Who's there?'
'Howl.'
'Howl who?'
'Howl you know unless you open the door?'

'Knock, knock.'
'Who's there?'
'Isaac.'
'Isaac who?'
'Isaac coming in!'

'Knock, knock.'
'Who's there?'
'Ivan.'
'Ivan who?'
'Ivan to come in!'

'Knock, knock.'
'Who's there?'
'Ivor.'
'Ivor who?'
'Ivor sore hand from knocking on your door!'

'Knock, knock.'
'Who's there?'
'Ivor.'
'Ivor who?'
'Ivor you let me in the door or I'll come through the window!'

'Knock, knock.'
'Who's there?'
'Lena.'
'Lena who?'
'Lean a little closer and I'll tell you!'

'Knock, knock.'
'Who's there?'
'Luke.'
'Luke who?'
'Luke through the keyhole and you'll find out!'

'Knock, knock.'
'Who's there?'
'Madam.'
'Madam who?'
'Madam finger's caught in the door!'

'Knock, knock.'
'Who's there?'
'Olivia.'
'Olivia who?'
'Olivia but I've lost my key!'

'Knock, knock.'
'Who's there?'
'Radio.'
'Radio who?'
'Radio not, here I come!'

'Knock, knock.'
'Who's there?'
'Repeat.'
'Repeat who?'
'Who, who, who, who . . .'

'Knock, knock.'
'Who's there?'
'Senior.'
'Senior who?'
'Senior so nosy, I'm not going to tell you!'

'Knock, knock.'
'Who's there?'
'Toodle.'
'Toodle who?'
'Toodle-oo to you too!'

'Knock, knock.'
'Who's there?'
'You.'
'You who?'
'Did you call?'

'Will you remember me in a week?'
'Yes.'
'Will you remember me in a month?'
'Yes.'
'Will you remember me in a year?'
'Yes.'
'Knock, knock.'
'Who's there?'
'Forgotten me already?'

L

Lavatories *See* **Toilets**.

Lawyers

What do lawyers wear in court?
Lawsuits.

What did the lawyer call his baby daughter?
Sue.

Ninety-nine per cent of lawyers give the rest a bad name.

An ethical lawyer and an honest politician fall out of an aeroplane together. Which of them hits the ground first? Don't be silly – they don't exist!

What do you get if you cross a godfather with a lawyer?
An offer you can't understand.

Two criminals hold up a group of lawyers in a bar. As they make their getaway the criminals check their takings. 'We got £50,' one says with a grin. The other frowns: 'But we went in there with £75!'

What is the difference between a leech and a lawyer?
A leech falls off you when you die.

A lawyer opens the door of his expensive car, only for it to be smashed off by a passing lorry. When the police arrive the lawyer complains loudly about the damage: 'Just look what a mess that idiot's made of my car!' The police officer sighs. 'You lawyers are so materialistic, it makes me sick. All you can think about is your stupid car – you haven't even noticed that your left arm has been ripped off.' 'My left arm? Oh my God! Where's my Rolex?'

What's the difference between a lawyer and a vampire?
A vampire only sucks blood at night.

What is the difference between a lawyer and an onion?
You cry when you cut up an onion.

What do you have when a lawyer is buried up to his neck in sand?
Not enough sand.

What do you call a thousand lawyers at the bottom of the sea?
A start.

What is black and white and looks great round a lawyer's neck?
A Rottweiler.

How do you get a lawyer out of a tree?
Cut the rope.

How do you stop a lawyer drowning?
Take your foot off his head.

How else do you stop a lawyer drowning?
Shoot him before he hits the water.

The good news is that a busload of lawyers just went over a cliff. The bad news is that one of the seats was empty.

A man walks into a bar with an alligator on a lead. He beckons the barman over. 'Do you serve lawyers here?' 'We certainly do,' says the barman. 'Great. Get me a beer – and a lawyer for the 'gator.'

Why do they bury lawyers twenty feet down?
Because deep down they are all good blokes.

Old lawyers never die, they just lose their appeal.

Laziness

'It is better to have loafed and lost than never to have loafed at all.' *(James Thurber)*

Did you hear about the lazy vicar?
He refused to work if there was a Sunday in the week.

Did you hear about the lazy gardener?
He had his window boxes concreted over.

My dad works almost every day. He almost works on Monday, he almost works on Tuesday, he almost works on Wednesday . . .

Two men are lazing the afternoon away in a bar. The first man turns to his friend and says, 'I was thinking I might go to Australia one day. I heard that if you go into the Outback there are diamonds just lying on the ground, waiting to be collected. All you have to do is bend down and pick them up.' The other goggles at him: 'Bend down?'

Letters

What travels the world but stays in one corner?
A stamp.

What did the stamp say to the envelope?
'Stick with me and we'll go places.'

How do you stick down an envelope underwater?
With a seal.

What's white on the outside and grey on the inside?
An elephant hiding inside an envelope.

Why did the dumb blonde keep checking her letter box for letters?
The computer kept telling her she had mail.

Libraries

Why did the bookworm go to the library?
He wanted to burrow a book.

Why can you never find a pink book in a library?
It's always taken to be red.

Why did the librarian slip on the library floor?
She was in the non-friction section.

Did you hear what happened when the man went into a library and asked where the self-help section was?
They told him he would have to find it himself.

'He said, "I'm going to chop off the bottom of one of your trouser legs and put it in a library." I thought, "That's a turn-up for the books." ' *(Tommy Cooper)*

See also **Book titles**; **Literature**.

Lies

'Doctor, doctor, I can't stop telling lies!'
'I don't believe you.'

What is a fibula?
A small lie.

The only time a fisherman tells the truth is when he calls another fisherman a liar.

What do liars do when they die?
They lie still.

Why are ghosts no good at telling lies?
Because you can see straight through them.

Light bulbs

What did the little light bulb say to its mother?
'I wuv you watts and watts.'

How many men does it take to change a light bulb?
One. He holds the bulb and waits for the world to revolve around him.

How many real men does it take to change a light bulb?
None. Real men aren't afraid of the dark.

How many jugglers does it take to change a light bulb?
One. But you need at least three bulbs.

How many actors does it take to change a light bulb?
Only one. They won't share the spotlight.

How many film directors does it take to change a light bulb?
One, but he wants to do it twenty-three times.

How many poets does it take to change a light bulb?
Three. One to curse the darkness, one to light a candle and one to change the bulb.

How many surrealists does it take to change a light bulb?
Two. One to hold the giraffe and one to melt the toffee.

How many lawyers does it take to change a light bulb?
How many can you afford?

How many civil servants does it take to change a light bulb?
Twenty-eight. One to change the bulb and twenty-seven to do the paperwork.

How many economists does it take to screw in a light bulb?
None. If the light bulb really needed changing, market forces would have already caused it to happen.

How many social scientists does it take to change a light bulb?

They do not change light bulbs: they search for the root cause as to why the last one went out.

How many psychologists does it take to change a light bulb?

One, but the light bulb really has to want to change.

How many dumb blondes does it take to change a light bulb?

Four hundred and three. One to hold the bulb and 402 to turn the room.

How many folk singers does it take to change a light bulb?

Two. One to change the bulb and one to write a song about how good the old one was.

'Do you know how many musicians it takes to change a light bulb?'

'No, but you hum it and I'll play it.'

'How many witches does it take to change a light bulb?'

'Into what?'

'Doctor, doctor, I've swallowed a light bulb!'

'Spit it out, then, and you'll be delighted.'

Limericks

There was a young man of Japan
Whose limericks never would scan;
When they said it was so,
He replied, 'Yes, I know,

But I always try to get as many words into the last line as
ever I possibly can.'

There once was a man from Peru
Whose limericks always end on line two.

Lions

What do you call a lion with no eyes?
A lon.

What kind of lion is perfectly harmless?
A dandelion.

How do lions keep up to date?
They watch the gnus.

A lion and a tiger are walking down the High Street. The
lion turns to the tiger and says, 'Not many people around
for a Saturday, are there?'

What's the difference between a lion with toothache and a
wet day?
One roars with pain and the other pours with rain.

A lion meets a leopard in the jungle and snarls menacingly
at him. 'Who is the King of the Jungle?' the lion growls.
'You are,' says the leopard hastily as it backs away. Next
the lion meets a monkey. 'Who is the King of the Jungle?'
the lion roars. 'You are,' says the monkey quickly and runs
up a tree. Next the lion meets an elephant. 'Who is the
King of the Jungle?' demands the lion once again. The
elephant picks up the lion with his trunk and hurls him
repeatedly against a tree before dropping him in a heap in

a patch of bramble. 'All right, all right,' gasps the lion, 'no need to lose your temper just because you don't know the answer!'

What do you get if you cross a dog and a lion?
A terrified postman.

Did you hear about the famous lion-hunter who always shot his prey between the eyes?
He was eaten by two one-eyed lions walking arm in arm.

Literature

'Outside of a dog, a book is probably man's best friend; inside of a dog, it's too dark to read.' *(Groucho Marx)*

What has a spine but no bones?
A book.

'Do you like Kipling?'
'I don't know – I've never kippled.'

A hungry lion comes across two men in the jungle. One is sitting on a log reading a book, while the other is working at a typewriter. Which one does the lion eat?
The reader, of course – even lions know that readers digest and writers cramp.

*See also **Book titles**; **Libraries**.*

Looks *See **Ugliness**.*

Lotteries See *Gambling*.

Love

'Knock, knock.'
'Who's there?'
'Aardvark.'
'Aardvark who?'
'Aardvark a hundred miles for one of your smiles.'

What happened when the two candles fell in love?
They met their match.

Did you hear about the two blood cells who fell in love?
They loved in vein.

Did you hear about the ghost and the vampire who fell in love?
It was love at first fright.

What did the one-eyed Cyclops say to his girlfriend?
'You are the one-eye adore.'

There was a young lady named Stella
Fell in love with a bow-legged fella.
The venturesome chap
Let her sit on his lap
And she plummeted down to the cellar.

See also **Dating**; **Marriage**; **Sex**.

M

Madness *See* **Insanity**.

Magicians

What do you get if you cross a snake with a magician?
An abra da cobra.

What did the fishmonger say to the magician?
'Pick a cod, any cod.'

What do you call a female magician?
Trixie.

What did one magician say to the other?
'Who was that girl I sawed you with last night?'

Manners

'If an Englishman gets run down by a truck, he apologizes
to the truck.' *(Jackie Mason)*

I sat next to the Duchess at tea,
Distressed as a person could be.
Her rumblings abdominal
Were simply phenomenal –
And everyone thought it was me!

There was a young man called Art
Who thought he'd be terribly smart,
He ate ten cans of beans,
And busted his jeans,
With a loud and earth-shattering fart.

Which hand should you use to stir your tea?
Neither. Use a spoon.

A precocious young lady named Lillian
Protruded her tongue at a Chilean;
Her mother said, pleading,
'Remember your breeding,
That trick is distinctly reptilian.'

Why are sausages rude?
Because they spit at you when you cook them.

There was an old man of Ealing
Who had an expectorant feeling.
But a sign on the door
Said 'Don't spit on the floor',
So he looked up and spat on the ceiling.

Why do rocks never say thank you?
They take everything for granite.

How do you cure a shy pebble?
Persuade it to be a little boulder.

Marriage

Why is a room full of married people empty?
There isn't a single person in it.

'I knew a man who married his sister.'
'Isn't that against the law?'
'No – he's a vicar.'

What is the difference between a married man and a
bachelor?
One kisses the missus and the other misses the kisses.

'Last week I took the first step towards getting divorced.'
'What did you do?'
'I got married.'

Why shouldn't you marry a tennis player?
Because love means nothing to them.

Marriage is the process of finding out what kind of man
your wife would have preferred.

'A man in love is incomplete until he's married. Then he's
finished.' *(Zsa Zsa Gabor)*

Why is a wedding ring like a tourniquet for a bachelor?
It stops his circulation.

Getting married is like going to a restaurant with friends.
You order what you want, then you see what the other
fellow has and wish you had ordered that.

'I think men who have pierced ears are better prepared for
marriage. They have experienced pain and bought
jewellery.' *(Rita Rudner)*

Ronnie Corbett Do you think marriage is a lottery?
Ronnie Barker No. With a lottery you do have a slight
chance.

What is the longest sentence known to man?
'I do.'

'Marriage is a wonderful institution, but who wants to live in an institution?' *(Groucho Marx)*

See also **Bigamy**; **Divorce**; **Husbands and wives**.

Mathematics

There are three kinds of people in the world. Those who can count, and those who can't.

Mathematics is 50 per cent formulas, 50 per cent proofs and 50 per cent imagination.

Why was the maths book sad?
Because it had so many problems.

Which sea creature is best at mathematics?
The octoplus.

Why is long division such hard work?
Because of all the numbers you have to carry.

Have you heard that $\frac{9}{8}$ths of people are hopeless at fractions?

Is it 'nine and five is thirteen' or 'nine and five are thirteen'?
Neither. Nine and five are fourteen.

Why is twice ten the same as twice eleven?
Because twice ten is twenty, and twice eleven is twenty too.

Teacher If I gave you three rabbits and then the next day I gave you five more, how many rabbits would you have?
Pupil Nine, miss.
Teacher Nine?
Pupil I've got one already.

Teacher If you had £5 in one pocket and £5 in the other pocket, what would you have?
Pupil Someone else's trousers on.

Teacher If you had ten chocolates and I took away four, what would you have?
Pupil A fight.

Teacher If your father borrowed £10 off me and he paid me back at £1 a month, how much would he owe me after six months?
Pupil £10.
Teacher You don't know much about subtraction!
Pupil You don't know much about my father!

Teacher If your dad earned £1000 a week and gave you half, what would you have?
Pupil A heart attack.

Teacher If eggs were 20p a dozen, how many would you get for 5p?
Pupil None.
Teacher None?
Pupil None. If I had 5p I'd get some sweets.

Teacher If I had eight apples in my right hand and nine apples in my left hand, what would I have?
Pupil Huge hands.

Teacher What is half of eight?
Pupil Up and down or across?
Teacher What do you mean?
Pupil Up and down, it's nought. Across, it's three.

Teacher What is half of infinity?
Pupil -nity.

A farmer and a small boy are gazing at a flock of sheep in a field. 'How many do you think there are?' asks the farmer. 'Six hundred and seventeen,' says the boy after a few seconds. 'That's amazing!' exclaims the farmer. 'That's absolutely right! How did you count them so quickly?' 'Easy,' says the boy, 'I just counted the legs and divided by four.'

See also **Numbers**.

Men

Why were males created before females?
Because you always need a rough draft before the final copy.

What do you call a good-looking, intelligent, sensitive man?
A rumour.

What do you call a man with half a brain?
Gifted.

Why are men like lava lamps?
They're fun to look at but not all that bright.

Why are men like bank accounts?
Without a lot of money, they don't generate much interest.

'Men forget everything; women remember everything. That's why men need instant replays in sports. They've already forgotten what happened.' *(Rita Rudner)*

Men have only two faults.
Everything they say and everything they do.

How many men does it take to change a roll of toilet paper?
No one knows – it's never happened.

What is the thinnest book in the world?
What Men Know About Women.

What's the difference between a man and E.T.?
E.T. phoned home.

What should you give a man who has everything?
A woman to show him how to work it.

What can do the work of five men?
One woman.

Why do men like clever women?
Because opposites attract.

What's the easiest way to kill a man?
Put a beautiful blonde and a beer in front of him and tell him to pick just one.

See also **Women**.

Mice

Did you hear about the baby mouse who saw a bat?
He ran to his mother and told her he had seen an angel.

What's the definition of a narrow squeak?
A thin mouse.

What do mice do during the daytime?
Mousework.

What do mice do when they move house?
Hold a mouse-warming party.

What kind of musical instrument do mice play?
A mouse organ.

What is a mouse's favourite game?
Hide and squeak.

What do angry mice send each other at Christmas?
Crossmouse cards.

Hickory hickory dock,
The mouse ran up the clock,
The clock struck one
But the rest got away with minor injuries.

How can you save a drowning mouse?
Mouse-to-mouse resuscitation.

A mouse in her room woke Miss Dowd,
Who was frightened and screamed very loud.
Then a happy thought hit her –
To scare off the critter
She sat up in bed and miaowed.

Why did the mouse fall over after it had been cut in half?
Because a mouse divided against itself cannot stand.

An elephant met a mouse in the jungle. 'Gosh,' said the
mouse, 'you're enormous!' 'Wow,' said the elephant,
'you're tiny!' 'Well,' said the mouse, 'I haven't been very
well lately.'

What do you get if you cross a bottle of washing-up liquid
with a mouse?
Bubble and squeak.

Mindreaders *See* Psychics.

Money

'I've worked myself up from nothing to a state of extreme
poverty.' *(Groucho Marx)*

Why is money called dough?
Because everyone kneads it.

Why can't you make a million pounds laugh?
Because it's serious money.

Mother Why did you just swallow the money I gave you?
Son Well, you did say it was my lunch money!

Daughter Can I have a pound for being good?
Father No, you can be good-for-nothing.

How much do pirates pay for their earrings?
A buccaneer.

Two bank managers watch a woman pass by with a £50 note in each ear. One turns to the other and says, 'See that woman? She's £100 in arrears.'

'Money can't buy you friends, but you get a better class of enemy.' *(Spike Milligan)*

Why should you always borrow money from pessimists? They don't expect you to pay it back.

'You owe me a pound for that honey.'
'What honey?'
'I never knew you cared!'

What's the difference between a forged pound note and an insane rabbit?
One is bad money and the other is a mad bunny.

What happened when the cat swallowed a coin?
There was some money in the kitty!

'I have enough money to last me the rest of my life. Unless I buy something.' *(Jackie Mason)*

'I wasn't always rich. There was a time I didn't know where my next husband was coming from.' *(Mae West)*

See also **Accountants**; **Taxation**.

Monkeys

What monkey can fly?
A hot air baboon.

What do you call a monkey sitting on a cake?
A marzipanzee.

What is the smallest monkey in the jungle called?
A shrimpanzee.

Why did the monkey fall out of the tree?
Because it was dead.
Why did the second monkey fall out of the tree?
Because it was dead too.
Why did the third monkey fall out of the tree?
Peer pressure . . .

Why did the warthog fall out of the tree?
It was doing a monkey impression.

What do you get if you cross a monkey with some egg whites?
A meringue-utan.

What do baby apes sleep in?
Apricots.

How do you fix a broken chimp?
With a monkey wrench.

See also **Gorillas**.

Monsters

'Knock, knock.'
'Who's there?'
'Turner.'
'Turner who?'
'Turn around, there's a monster behind you!'

'Knock, knock.'
'Who's there?'
'Lucretia.'
'Lucretia who?'
'Lucretia from the Black Lagoon.'

What is the best way to talk to a monster?
From a long way off.

How does a monster count to fifteen?
On its fingers.

Did you hear about the monster who had twenty arms
and no legs?
He was all fingers and thumbs.

Why are monsters' fingers never more than eleven inches
long?
Because if they were twelve inches long they would be a
foot.

Which monsters have the best hearing?
The eeriest.

Why are monsters forgetful?
Everything goes in one ear and out the others.

First monster Nerg.
Second monster Nerg, nerg, gug.
First monster Don't change the subject.

What do sea monsters eat?
Fish and ships.

How do monsters like their food cooked?
Terror-fried.

What do monsters like to drink?
Slime cordial.

What was the ten-foot monster called?
Shorty.

Did you hear about the monster who had to have an operation?
He had his ghoul-stones removed.

Why did the monster cut off the top of his head?
He wanted to keep an open mind.

What happened to the monster who swallowed a clock?
He got ticks.

Which monster is the cleverest?
Frank-Einstein.

Why was Dr Frankenstein never lonely?
He was good at making friends.

Which is the unluckiest monster in the world?
The Luck Less Monster.

What do you call a good-looking, kind, friendly monster?
A failure.

'What has a purple body, huge fangs, hairy legs and eyes on stalks?'
'I don't know. What has a purple body, huge fangs, hairy legs and eyes on stalks?'
'I don't know either – but there's one crawling up your leg.'

Why couldn't the monster get to sleep?
He thought there were humans under the bed.

Why did the monster bring toilet paper to the party?
He was a party pooper.

See also **Abominable snowmen**; **Dragons**; **Ghosts**;
Mummies; **Skeletons**; **Vampires**; **Werewolves**;
Zombies.

Mothers-in-law

Behind every successful man stands a surprised
mother-in-law.

Did you hear about the mother-in-law who complimented
her daughter's husband?
She called him a perfect idiot.

Why did the dog owner have his dog's tail cut off?
His mother-in-law was coming the next day and he didn't
want anything to make her think she was welcome.

'The wife's mother said, "When you're dead, I'll dance
on your grave." I said, "Good, I'm being buried at sea." '
(Les Dawson)

Mixed feelings is when you see your mother-in-law drive
over a cliff in your new car.

'The wife's mother said, "How would you like to have a
chat with me?" I said, "Through a medium." ' *(Les Dawson)*

A hunter is on safari with his wife and his mother-in-law
when the mother-in-law gets separated and cornered by a

hungry lion. 'Quick!' the wife shouts to her husband. 'Do something!' 'No way!' says the hunter. 'The lion got himself into this mess. He can get himself out of it.'

Moths

What is the biggest moth of all?
A mammoth.

What is a myth?
A female moth.

What subject do moths study at school?
Mothematics.

Which insect can tell your fortune?
A gypsy moth.

Why was the moth so unpopular?
He kept picking holes in everything!

'Doctor, doctor, I think I'm a moth.'
'Why come round and tell me?'
'Well, I saw this light at the window . . .'

See also **Butterflies**.

Motorists

What was the name of the Spaniard who couldn't find his car?
Carlos.

What do you call a man under a car?
Jack.

'So I was getting into my car, and this bloke says to me, "Can you give me a lift?" I said, "Sure – you look great, the world's your oyster, go for it."' *(Tommy Cooper)*

A motorist stops to ask another driver who has broken down if he can lend a hand. 'No thanks,' comes the reply, 'I'm waiting for a toe.'

A woman motorist greets her husband at the door when he gets home. 'I've got good news and bad news about the car,' she says. 'The good news is that the air bag works.'

A man having a snack in a motorway service station is accosted by three aggressive Hell's Angels who spit in his coffee, knock his food on the floor and push him off his chair. Instead of retaliating, the man just walks out. 'He's not much of a man!' one of the bikers tells the waitress. 'He's not much of a driver either,' replies the waitress. 'He's just driven his lorry over three bikes.'

A police officer stops a driver who has been speeding and asks why he was going so fast. 'Well,' the driver explains, 'my brakes aren't working properly and I wanted to get home before I had an accident.'

Newsflash: A tanker has spilt its load of glue on the motorway. Drivers are advised to stick to the inside lane.

Old motorists never die, they just lose their drive.

See also **Cars**; **Traffic wardens**.

Mummies

Why was the Egyptian girl confused?
Because her daddy was a mummy.

What do mummies put on their fingernails?
Nile varnish.

What does a mummy do when he is angry?
He flips his lid.

What kind of music do mummies like?
Wrap music.

Music

What note do you get if you drop a piano down a mine shaft?
A flat minor (miner).

What do you get if you drop a piano on an army barracks?
A flat major.

Why couldn't the pianist open his piano?
The keys were inside.

Teacher You two boys, how are you at picking up music?
Pupils Brilliant, miss.
Teacher Right, move that piano.

What do a viola and a lawsuit have in common?
Everyone is happy when the case is closed.

How do you get two viola players to play in perfect unison?
Shoot one of them.

Why did the musician keep his trumpet in the fridge?
He liked cool music.

'A strange thing happened during a performance of Elgar's *Sea Pictures* at a concert hall in Bermuda tonight. The man playing the triangle disappeared.' *(Ronnie Barker)*

What are the most musical parts of a turkey?
The drumsticks.

Small boy Mummy, I want to be a drummer when I grow up!
Mummy Now, dear, you know perfectly well you can't do both.

Why do bagpipers walk when they play?
They want to get away from the noise.

What is the definition of a gentleman?
A man who knows how to play the bagpipes, but doesn't.

What kind of music does a fish listen to?
Soul music.

What kind of music do ghosts like best?
Haunting melodies.

There was a young girl in the choir
Whose voice went up higher and higher,
Till one Sunday night
It vanished from sight
And turned up next day in the spire.

What's green and sings?
Elvis Parsley.

What has forty feet and sings?
A school choir.

'My wife's gone on a singing tour of South Korea.'
'Seoul?'
'No, rhythm and blues.'

A charming young singer named Hannah
Got caught in a flood in Savannah;
As she floated away,
Her sister, they say,
Accompanied her on the piannah.

Why was the musician arrested?
He got into treble.

What do you call a musician who doesn't have a
girlfriend?
Homeless.

Music teacher If *f* means *forte*, what does *ff* mean?
Pupil Eighty?

How do you make a bandstand?
Take away their chairs.

What do you call a part-time bandleader?
A semi-conductor.

Which fish is the most musical?
The piano-tuna.

What is Beethoven doing these days?
Decomposing.

How did the musician remember what he had to get when
he went shopping?
He wrote a Chopin Liszt.

How does the sky listen to music?
Through a cloudspeaker.

'I'm not playing all the wrong notes. I'm playing all
the right notes. But not necessarily in the right order.'
(Eric Morecambe)

What do you get if you cross a hen with a guitar?
A chicken that plucks itself.

'I don't like country music, but I don't mean to denigrate
those who do. And for the people who like country music,
denigrate means "put down".' *(Bob Newhart)*

'Doctor, doctor, I've swallowed a trumpet!'
'Let me take a few notes.'

'Doctor, doctor, I've swallowed my harmonica!'
'Be thankful you don't play the piano.'

'Doctor, doctor, I can't stop singing "The Green, Green
Grass of Home"!'
'That sounds like Tom Jones syndrome.'
'Is it common?'
'It's not unusual.'

N

Names

'Knock, knock.'
'Who's there?'
'Avenue.'
'Avenue who?'
'Avenue learned my name yet?'

Small boy Mummy, I'm really glad you decided to call me Adam.
Mother Why's that?
Small boy Because that's what everyone calls me at school as well.

What do you call a Chinese woman with a food processor on her head?
Brenda.

What do you call a man with a seagull on his head?
Cliff.

When twins came, their father John Dunn
Gave 'Edward' as name to each son.
When folks said: 'Absurd!'
He replied: 'Haven't you heard
That two Eds are better than one?'

What do you call a woman with one leg?
Eileen.
What do you call a Chinese lady with one leg?
Irene.

What do you call a man who relies on government handouts?
Grant.

What was the name of the Russian Pepsi delivery man?
Idropalotofpopoff.

Why did the farmer call his pig Ink?
Because he kept running out of the pen.

What do you call a man with sports equipment on his head?
Jim.

What do you call a man who wears a coat?
Mac.
What do you call a man who wears two coats?
Max.

What do you call a woman tied up at a jetty?
Maude.

What do you call a man with no legs?
Neil.

What do you call a man who is deeply in debt?
Owen.

What do you call a man buried in a garden?
Pete.

What was the name of the Italian with a rubber toe?
Roberto.

What do you call a man with three eyes?
Seymour.

What do you call a man in a cooking pot?
Stu.

What do you call a man with a rabbit on his head?
Warren.

'Going to call him William? What kind of a name is that?
Every Tom, Dick and Harry's called William. Why don't
you call him Bill?' *(Samuel Goldwyn)*

Why did the Welsh couple name their fifth child Yin Li?
They'd heard that every fifth baby born in the world is
Chinese.

Neighbours

A wife is much impressed by the loving behaviour of the
couple next door. One evening she rounds on her
husband and demands, 'Do you see that couple? How
devoted they are? He kisses her whenever they meet. Why
don't you do that?' 'I'd love to,' replies the husband, 'but I
don't know her well enough.'

First neighbour Can I borrow your lawn-mower?
Second neighbour No, she's out.

First neighbour Did you hear me banging on the wall last
night?

Second neighbour Don't worry. We were making quite a lot of noise ourselves.

An old lady complains to the police about her neighbour, who walks around the house naked with the curtains open. 'But, madam,' says the police officer as he peers from the old lady's window at the offending house, 'you can't see into his house from here.' 'No,' replies the old lady, 'you have to climb onto the bookcase and look through the skylight.'

Noah's ark

'Knock, knock.'
'Who's there?'
'Noah.'
'Noah who?'
'Noah don't know who you are either.'

What was Noah's job?
He was an arkitect.

How did the animals see their way into the ark?
By floodlighting.

Why were the elephants last to board Noah's ark?
They took so long to pack their trunks.

What were the only creatures that did not go into Noah's ark in pairs?
Maggots. They went in an apple.

Was Noah first to come out of the ark?
No, he came forth out of the ark.

What did Noah call his daughter?
Joan of Ark.

Nudity

Why did the traffic light turn red?
It had to change in the middle of the street.

What do you call a pig with no clothes on?
Streaky bacon.

Why did the married couple go to a nudist camp?
To air their differences.

Two children are spying on some nudists. 'Which are the women and which are the men?' one asks. 'I don't know,' says the other, 'they haven't got their clothes on.'

Newsflash: A hole has been found in the wall of a nudist colony. The police are looking into it.

Numbers

What did the 0 say to the number 8?
'Nice belt!'

Why was six scared of seven?
Because seven eight nine.

What should you take from seven to make it even?
The S.

Why is nine drunk?
Because it is one over the eight.

See also **Mathematics**.

Nuns *See* **Religion**.

Nuts

Why did the peanut complain to the police?
Because he had been assaulted.

What kind of nuts are always sneezing?
Cashews.

What kind of nut grows on walls?
Walnuts.

How do you know that peanuts are fattening?
Have you ever seen a skinny elephant?

See also **Food**.

O

Octopuses

What does an octopus wear in cold weather?
A coat of arms.

What do you call a neurotic octopus?
A crazy, mixed-up squid.

How could the octopus afford a house?
He prawned everything.

How does an octopus go into battle?
Fully armed.

What happened to the octopus who deserted the army?
He faced a firing squid.

If you had three octopuses in your wallet how rich would you be?
Squids in.

Old age See **Age**.

Owls

Why did the owl 'owl?
Because the woodpecker would peck 'er.

What noise do owls make when it is raining?
'Too wet to woo.'

What did the stupid owl say?
'What, what?'

What subject are owls best at?
Owlgebra.

P

Parachuting See **Extreme sports**.

Parents

My parents know nothing about children. When I'm wide awake they make me go to bed and when I'm sleepy they make me get up!

A small boy is out with his father. 'Daddy,' he asks, 'why does it get dark?' 'I don't know,' replies Daddy. 'Daddy,' says the small boy after a moment or two, 'where do the stars come from?' 'I don't know,' says Daddy. 'Daddy,' says the small boy a little later, 'how do birds know their way home?' 'I don't know,' says Daddy. 'Daddy,' says the small boy, 'do you mind me asking all these questions?' 'Of course not,' says Daddy, 'if you don't ask questions how will you ever learn anything?'

What is the difference between a Rottweiler and a Jewish mother?
The Rottweiler eventually lets go.

What does a zombie call his parents?
Mummy and Deady.

*See also **Children**; **Families**; **Grandparents**.*

Parrots

What do parrots eat?
Polyfilla.

Why do parrots wear raincoats?
So they can stay polyunsaturated.

What do you call a Scottish parrot?
A Macaw.

Two parrots are sitting on a perch. One turns to the other and says, 'Can you smell fish?'

Who would you call to treat a poorly parrot?
A parrot-medic.

Why can't you get aspirins in the jungle?
Because the parrots eat 'em all.

A young woman walks into a pub with a parrot on her shoulder. 'Goodness,' says the landlord, 'where did you get that good-looking bird?' 'Usual place,' says the parrot, 'internet chat room.'

Why are parrots so clever?
Because they suck seed (succeed).

What do you get if you cross a parrot with a centipede?
A walkie-talkie.

What do you get if you cross a parrot with a shark?
A bird that will talk your ear off.

What do you get if you cross a parrot with an elephant?
Something that tells everything it remembers.

Parties

'Knock, knock.'
'Who's there?'
'Justin.'
'Justin who?'
'Justin time for the party.'

What game do cows play at parties?
Moosical chairs.

What game do young ghosts play at parties?
Haunt the thimble.

A man goes to a fancy-dress party with a girl on his back.
'I've come as a snail,' he announces. 'Why the girl on your
back?' the other guests ask. 'That's Michelle.'

There was a young man from Bengal
Who was asked to a fancy-dress ball.
He said he would risk it
And went as a biscuit,
But a dog ate him up in the hall.

Pets

Do you know why I keep my pet newt in a matchbox?
Because it's my newt.

What pet makes the most noise?
A trumpet.

Customer at pet shop Do you have any dogs going cheap?
Sales assistant No, only ones that go 'woof'.

Pupil Can I bring my three dogs to school?
Teacher What about the noise and the mess?
Pupil Oh, they won't mind.

Mother Have you changed the water in the goldfish bowl?
Child No, they haven't drunk the last lot yet.

Pigs

Why is getting up in the morning like a pig's tail?
Because it's twirly (too early).

What kind of tie do pigs wear?
A pig-sty.

Why don't pigs ever go on holiday?
They prefer to sty at home.

Why do baby pigs eat so much?
They want to make hogs of themselves.

What do you call a pig that does karate?
A pork chop.

Why was the pig arrested?
He didn't have a grunting licence.

Why can't pigs keep secrets?
Because they are squealers.

How do pigs write letters?
With pen and oink.

Why did the pig go on strike?
He felt he was being taken for grunted.

What do you give a sick pig?
Oinkment.

Why do sick pigs always die?
Because they have to be killed before they are cured.

'That man said you weren't fit to associate with pigs, but I stuck up for you.'
'What did you say?'
'I said you were.'

What do you get if you cross a pig with a telephone?
Crackling on the line.

What do you get if you cross a pig with a box of itching powder?
Pork scratchings.

'Doctor, doctor, I think I'm turning into a pig!'
'How long have you felt like this?'
'A weeeeek.'

Plane travel See **Aviation**.

Polar bears

Penguin What's your name?
Polar bear My name is . . . Kevin.
Penguin Why the large pause?
Polar bear I've always had them.

What do polar bears have for lunch?
Ice burgers.

Where do polar bears vote?
The North Poll.

What do you call a hungry polar bear with a bad temper?
Sir.

See also **Bears**.

Police officers

'Knock, knock.'
'Who's there?'
'Police.'
'Police who?'
'Police open the door.'

Why do police officers have numbers?
In case they get lost.

What did the burglar say when arrested by a blonde police officer?
'It's a fair cop.'

Who do they send for if someone commits a crime underwater?
The plaice.

What is the address of the police station?
999 Letsby Avenue.

Did you hear what the detective said to the man who walked down the street carrying a computer, a swivel chair, a table and a potted plant?
'I'm arresting you for impersonating an office, sir.'

'Police arrested two kids yesterday. One was drinking battery acid, the other was eating fireworks. They charged one and let the other off.' *(Tommy Cooper)*

Newsflash: A lorryload of mattresses have been stolen. The police are springing into action.

A police patrol car is overtaken by a car driven at high speed by a woman busy knitting. The police officer lowers his window and shouts, 'Pull over!' The woman shakes her head and yells back: 'No – socks!'

'The search for the man who terrorizes nudist camps with a bacon slicer goes on. Inspector Lemuel Jones had a tip-off this morning, but hopes to be back on duty tomorrow.' *(Ronnie Barker)*

Old police officers never die, they just cop out.

See also **Burglars**; **Criminals**; **Gangsters**.

Politics

Why do anarchists drink cheap tea?
Because all proper tea is theft.

'The prime minister held a meeting with the cabinet today. He also spoke to the bookcase and argued with the chest of drawers.' *(Ronnie Barker)*

Newsflash: Early this morning the personal library of President George W. Bush was destroyed by fire. Both books were lost in the blaze. Sadly, due to his hectic schedule, the president had not had time to colour in the second one.

How many politicians does it take to change a light bulb?
Two. One to change it, and another one to change it back again.

How many spin doctors does it take to change a light bulb?
Four. One to change it and the other three to deny it.

How many Marxists does it take to change a light bulb?
None. The seeds of change are within the light bulb itself.

What's the difference between the government and the Mafia?
One of them is organized.

'Too bad all the people who know how to run the country are busy driving cabs and cutting hair.' *(George Burns)*

Post See *Letters*.

Prison

What do prisoners use to call each other?
Cell phones.

What's the difference between a gaoler and a jeweller?
One watches cells and the other sells watches.

What do you call a snobbish convict coming down a staircase?
A condescending con descending.

A group of prisoners have been in prison so long they know each other's jokes by heart. To save time, they refer to them by number. One prisoner says, 'Number seventeen,' and everyone smiles. Another says, 'Remember number five?' and everyone chuckles. A third prisoner responds with, 'How about that number eleven, eh?' and everyone grins. One prisoner, however, is rolling on the floor in helpless laughter at this one. Eventually, he recovers and shrugs apologetically to his friends: 'Sorry, that's the first time I heard that one.'

Three prisoners are sentenced to twenty years behind bars. Each is allowed one item to keep in their cell. The first prisoner asks for a pile of law books. The second prisoner asks for his wife. The third prisoner asks for two hundred cigarettes. After twenty years they are all released. The first says, 'Thank God for those books. I have now passed all my law exams and can practise as a highly paid lawyer.' The second says, 'Thank God for my wife. Now I have five children and a settled family life to look forward to.' The third says, 'Anyone got a match?'

See also **Burglars**; **Courts of law**; **Criminals**; **Executions**; **Judges**.

Pronunciation

What word do people always pronounce wrong?
Wrong.

A woman goes into the butcher's and asks for a steak and kidley pie. 'Don't you mean steak and kidney?' replies the butcher. 'That's what I said, diddle I?'

Pupil Ow! I just banged my fumb!
Teacher Thumb, boy, not fumb.
Pupil I know – and I banged my thinger as well!

'Doctor, doctor, I can't pronounce my Fs, Ts or Hs.'
'Well, you can't say fairer than that.'

Psychiatrists

Why did Cleopatra refuse to see a psychiatrist?
She was the Queen of Denial.

Why did the monster go to the psychiatrist?
Because he thought everybody loved him.

Why do psychiatrists like to treat schizophrenics?
They can charge them double.

Did you hear about the man who went to the psychiatrist
complaining of an irresistible impulse to kill himself?
The psychiatrist insisted that he pay in advance.

'Anyone who goes to a psychiatrist ought to have his head
examined.' *(Samuel Goldwyn)*

See also **Insanity**.

Psychics

Why did the psychic cross the road?
To reach the other side.

What did the psychic say to the other psychic?
'You're fine. How am I?'

Did you hear about the psychics' meeting the other night?
It was cancelled due to unforeseen circumstances.

How did the psychic know what he was getting for
Christmas?
He felt his presents.

Why did the man punch the psychic when she started
laughing?
He was striking a happy medium.

A short psychic escaped from prison. The newspaper
headline read, 'Small medium at large.'

Did you hear about the woman who bought an old crystal
ball for £50?
They must have seen her coming.

Did you hear about the man who decided to consult a
psychic for the first time?
When he knocked on the door the psychic called out,
'Who's there?' So the man left.

I nearly fell in love with a psychic, but she left me before
we met.

See also **Ghosts**.

Pubs

Why are criminals and pub landlords similar?
They both spend a lot of time behind bars.

A man walks into a bar and says 'Ouch!'
It was an iron bar.

A dyslexic man walks into a bra.

William Shakespeare walks into the pub and asks for a beer. 'Sorry,' says the landlord, 'I can't serve you. You're bard.'

A ghost walks into a pub and asks for a whisky. 'Sorry,' says the landlord, 'we don't serve spirits.'

A bag of chips walks into a pub and asks for a beer. 'I'm sorry,' says the landlord, 'we don't serve food.'

A man walks into a pub and orders a beer. He is just about to start drinking when the bowl of nuts on the bar tells him he is wearing a great shirt. Somewhat startled by this, the man moves away from the bar and sits next to a cigarette vending machine. As he raises his glass the vending machine suddenly starts screaming abuse at him. Thoroughly shaken, the man returns to the bar and complains to the landlord. The landlord apologizes and explains, 'The peanuts are complimentary, but the cigarette machine is out of order.'

A piece of string walks into a pub and orders a drink. 'Sorry,' says the landlord, 'we don't serve string.' The string goes outside, ties a knot in his neck, ruffles his hair and comes back in. 'I'd like a beer, please.' The landlord frowns. 'Aren't you that piece of string who came in just now?' 'No,' says the piece of string, 'I'm a frayed knot.'

A man goes into a pub with a lump of tarmac under his arm. 'A pint of beer, please,' he orders, 'and one for the road.'

Two pieces of black tarmac are sitting in a bar having a drinking contest to see which one is the hardest.

Suddenly, the door opens and a piece of red tarmac walks in. At this, one of the two pieces of black tarmac leaps up from his stool and rushes into the toilets. The piece of red tarmac drinks a beer and then leaves, upon which the piece of black tarmac cautiously returns to his stool. His companion asks why he ran off when the piece of red tarmac came in. 'Haven't you heard about him?' his friend replies. 'He's a cycle-path!'

Drinker Do you serve women here?
Landlord No, you have to bring your own.

Why did the ghost go to the pub after he lost the tail of his sheet in a revolving door?
He read the sign over the door saying they would retail spirits.

See also **Alcohol**.

Punctuality

Why was the brush late for work?
It over swept.

'Sorry I'm late. I was dreaming about a football match.'
'Why should that make you late?'
'They went into overtime.'

Boss You should have been here at nine!
Employee Why, what happened?

What did the electrician say to the other electrician when he turned up late for work?
'Wire you insulate?'

A factory worker has been having a lot of trouble getting up in the morning and is always late for work. His boss threatens to sack him if he doesn't start coming in on time, so the man goes to the doctor for help. The doctor gives him a pill and tells him to take it before he goes to bed. The man does as he is told and sleeps really well, waking up before the alarm has even gone off. He has time for a proper breakfast and is still one of the first to arrive at the factory. 'Boss,' he says, 'that pill really works!' 'I'm pleased to hear it,' says his boss, 'but where were you yesterday?'

Teacher Why are you always late for school?
Pupil Because you ring the bell before I get there.

See also **Absence**.

Puns

A good pun is its own reword.

A man enters a punning contest in the local paper. He sends in ten different puns and is confident one or other of them will win the competition. Unfortunately, no pun in ten did.

Two weevils live in the same biscuit. One of them grows very large and becomes quite a local celebrity. In comparison, the other weevil is puny and unknown – in fact, the lesser of two weevils.

A local decorator is paid £300 to repaint the interior of a church. He is too mean to spend it all on paint, so dilutes the paint with water. When he sees that the thinned paint will not cover all the walls he dilutes the paint even further. He still needs more, so decides to dilute the paint one more time. Just then a voice booms from the heavens: 'Stop! Repaint and thin no more!'

Mahatma Gandhi had badly calloused feet, frail health and bad breath. In other words, he was a super-calloused fragile mystic plagued with halitosis.

Why did the Mexican shoot at his wife?
Tequila.

R

Rabbits

What do you get if you pour hot water down a rabbit hole?
Hot cross bunnies.

What do rabbits do after they get married?
They go on bunnymoon.

Teacher If you had a rabbit in a hutch, and you bought another rabbit, how many rabbits would you have?
Pupil Ten.
Teacher You don't know your arithmetic.
Pupil You don't know my rabbits.

What is the difference between a jogging rabbit and a cross-eyed rabbit?
One is a fit bunny and the other's a bit funny.

What do you get if you cross a rabbit with a cake?
A cream bun.

How can you tell a rabbit from a gorilla?
They look different.

Where do rabbits learn to fly?
In the Hare Force.

What do you call a rich rabbit?
A millionhare.

What do you call a row of hares hopping backwards?
A receding hair line.

How did the beautician bring a dead hare back to life?
She used revitalizing hair spray.

Rail travel

How do trains hear?
Through their engineers.

Why did the train go 'ouch'?
Because it had a tender behind.

What kind of shoes do railway workers wear?
Platform shoes.

What's shut when it's open and open when it's shut?
A level crossing.

Where do ghost trains stop?
At manifestations.

Why are ghost trains so rare?
They only run on a skeleton service.

Religion

Did you hear about the couple who split up over their religious differences?
He thought he was God, but she didn't.

'Knock, knock.'
'Who's there?'
'Armageddon.'
'Armageddon who?'
'Armageddon out of here!'

What is the most religious insect?
A mosqueito.

What bit of fish doesn't make sense?
The piece of cod that passeth all understanding.

How do you make holy water?
Boil the hell out of it.

A gentle old lady I knew
Was dozing one day in her pew.
When the preacher yelled, 'Sin!'
She exclaimed, 'Count me in,
As soon as the service is through!'

A man joins a Trappist order and is told that he is allowed
to say just two words every five years. After five years he
speaks his two words to his superiors. 'Bed hard,' he says.
He is promised the problem will be looked into. Another
five years pass. This time his two words are: 'Food cold.'
Again his superiors promise to take care of the problem.
Five years later his two words are 'I quit.' His superiors
look at one another wearily. 'We're not the least bit
surprised. You've done nothing but complain for the last
fifteen years!'

'Why is it that when we talk to God we're said to be
praying, but when God talks to us we're schizophrenic?'
(Lily Tomlin)

Two priests are stopped by a police officer for speeding on a motorbike. 'What's the idea?' the police officer demands. 'You could have an accident going as fast as that.' One of the priests pats the police officer reassuringly on the arm. 'Don't alarm yourself, my son. Jesus is with us.' The police officer gets out his notebook. 'In that case, I'll have to book you. You can't have three people on a motorbike.'

What do you get if you cross an abbot with a trout?
A monkfish.

What do you get if you cross a monk with the moon?
A nocturnal habit.

What do you get if you cross an elephant with a nun?
A creature of habit.

What do you get if you cross a chicken with a nun?
A pecking order.

'If only God would give me some clear sign! Like making a large deposit in my name at a Swiss bank.' *(Woody Allen)*

'What is a hindu?'
'It lays eggs.'

What did the Buddhist say when he ordered a hot dog?
'Make me one with everything.'

Did you hear about the Buddhist who refused a painkiller at the dentist's?
He wanted to transcend dental medication.

'Not only is there no God, but try getting a plumber on weekends.' *(Woody Allen)*

See also **Vicars**.

Restaurants

What do you call the rear entrance to a cafeteria?
A bacteria.

A man is choosing something to eat from the menu in an Indian restaurant. 'What's this chicken tarka?' he asks. The waiter replies, 'It's like chicken tikka, but 'otter.'

A man orders a pizza at the restaurant. 'Would you like that cut into six pieces or twelve?' asks the waiter. 'Better make it six,' the man replies, 'I don't think I could manage twelve.'

A lady while dining at Crewe
Found an elephant's tail in her stew.
Said the waiter, 'Don't shout,
And wave it about,
Or the others will all want one too.'

'Knock, knock.'
'Who's there?'
'Waiter.'
'Waiter who?'
'Waiter minute while I tie my shoelaces up!'

See also **Cooking**; **Waiter, waiter**.

Riddles

When is a door not a door?
When it's ajar.

What gets wet as it dries?
A towel.

What's black and white and red all over?
A newspaper.

What's black when it's clean and white when it's dirty?
A blackboard.

What goes black, white, black, white, black, white?
A penguin rolling down an iceberg.

Now you see it, now you don't: what is it?
A black cat walking over a zebra crossing.

What is black and yellow and buzzes around at 400 miles
per hour?
A bee in an aeroplane.

What's red and white?
Pink.

What's pink and fluffy?
Pink fluff.
What's blue and fluffy?
Pink fluff holding its breath.

What is brown and sticky?
A stick.

What is round and violent?
A vicious circle.

What runs but never walks?
Water.

What's taken before you get it?
Your picture.

What grows bigger the more you take away?
A hole.

What can you keep and give away at the same time?
A cold.

What can you put in a cup but not take out again?
A crack.

What breaks when you say it?
Silence.

What can you hold without ever touching it?
A conversation.

What's pointed in one direction and headed in the other?
A pin.

What is full of holes but can hold water?
A sponge.

What goes up but doesn't come down?
Your age.

What goes up and down but never moves?
Stairs.

What goes further the slower it goes?
Money.

What flies but never goes anywhere?
A flag.

Which month of the year has twenty-eight days?
All of them.

What has four legs, whiskers, a tail and flies?
A dead cat.

What kind of animal has four legs and can see just as well at either end?
A horse with its eyes closed.

Which animals can you eat before they are born and after they're dead?
Chickens.

What has four legs and one foot?
A bed.

What has four legs but can't walk?
A table.

What has four legs and flies?
A picnic table.

What has eight legs and flies?
A dead donkey lying on a picnic table.

What has four legs, is big, green, fuzzy, and if it fell out of a tree would kill you?
A snooker table.

What has a bottom at the top?
Your legs.

What has a neck but no head?
A bottle.

What has four eyes and a mouth?
The Mississippi.

What is the difference between a duck?
One of its legs is both the same.

'Three boys called Peter, Paul and Pardon fell in the river.
Peter and Paul were drowned. Who was left?'
'Pardon.'
'Three boys called Peter, Paul and Pardon fell in the river.
Peter and Paul were drowned . . .'

Royalty

Why did the king go to the dentist?
To have his teeth crowned.

What is the difference between the Prince of Wales and a
tennis ball?
One is heir to the throne and the other is thrown in the
air.

Where was the Queen of England crowned?
On her head.

'Following the dispute with the domestic servants' union
at Buckingham Palace today, the Queen, a radiant figure
in a white silk gown and crimson robe, swept down the
main staircase and through the hall. She then dusted the
cloakroom and vacuumed the lounge.' *(Ronnie Barker)*

S

Sailors

Did you hear about the sailor who was discharged from the submarine service?
He slept with the window open.

Why did the sailor grab a bar of soap as he jumped off the sinking ship?
He hoped it would wash him ashore.

What stories do sailors tell their children?
Ferry tales.

Why do opera singers make bad sailors?
They hate the high Cs.

See also **Sea**; **Ships**.

Scarecrows *See* **Farming**.

School

The good news is that we are having only a half day at school this morning. The bad news is that we are having the other half this afternoon.

Why is a classroom like an old car?
Because it's full of nuts and has a crank at the front.

Mother How did you enjoy your first day at school?
Pupil First day? You mean I have to go back tomorrow?

Why didn't the little girl want to leave nursery school?
She wanted to be a nurse.

See also **Absence**; **Examinations**; **Geography**; **History**;
Homework; **Mathematics**; **Science**; **Teachers**.

School dinners *See* Cooking.

Science

Which weighs more, a ton of feathers or a ton of bricks?
Neither. They both weigh a ton.

What is as big as Big Ben but weighs nothing at all?
Big Ben's shadow.

What is bought by the metre and worn by the foot?
A carpet.

Which is fastest – cold or heat?
Heat, because you can catch cold.

Teacher Name a liquid that will not freeze.
Pupil Hot water.

Teacher Heat causes expansion and cold causes
contraction. Can someone give me an example of this?

Pupil Days are longer in summer when it's hot and shorter in winter when it's cold.

What goes up and down but doesn't move?
The temperature.

What is frozen water?
Ice.
What is frozen cream?
Ice cream.
What is frozen tea?
Iced tea.
What is frozen coffee?
Iced coffee.
What is frozen ink?
Iced ink.
You'd better have a bath then.

How long does a burning candle last?
About a wick.

What burns longer, a red candle or a green candle?
Neither. They both burn shorter.

If you breathe oxygen during the day, what do you breathe at night?
Nitrogen.

What is H_2O4?
Drinking.

Medical professor What happens when the human body is immersed in water?
Student The telephone rings.

Teacher Can anyone tell me a good way to save water?
Pupil Dilute it?

What is Cole's Law?
Thinly sliced cabbage.

What is the periodic table?
A table you use only occasionally.

What is copper nitrate?
Overtime pay for police officers.

There once was a lady, Eileen,
Who lived on distilled kerosene.
But she started absorbin'
A new hydrocarbon
And since then she's never benzene.

What is thick, black, floats on water and swears?
Crude oil.

What is black, gushes out of the ground and says, 'Excuse me'?
Refined oil.

How do you make antifreeze?
You hide her nightie.

Did you hear about the chemist who invented a solvent that would dissolve anything it came into contact with?
He couldn't find anything to keep it in.

Teacher Name one thing that conducts electricity.
Pupil Why – er . . .
Teacher Correct.

Two atoms meet in the street. One tells the other, 'Hey! I think I've lost an electron!' 'Are you sure?' 'Yes, I'm positive.'

What is a quark?
The noise a well-bred duck makes.

How long did Einstein live?
All his life.

There was a young lady named Bright
Whose speed was far faster than light.
She set off one day
In a relative way
And came back the previous night.

What is the centre of gravity?
V.

Why won't the Earth come to an end?
Because it's round.

A drunk loitering on a street corner is accosted by a police officer. 'What are you hanging about here for?' The drunk replies, 'I heard the world goes around every twenty-four hours, and I'm waiting for my house.'

How are genes inherited?
When they become too small for your older brother.

What was the microbe's mother called?
Minimum.

Old chemists never die, they just don't react any more.

Sea

What is the difference between see and sea?
You can see the sea but the sea can't see you.

'Did you hear the joke about the ocean?'
'It was too deep for me.'

What did the sea say to the sand?
Nothing. It just waved.

How did the beach get wet?
The sea weed.

How does seaweed find work?
It checks the kelp wanted ads in the paper.

What kind of hair do oceans have?
Wavy.

Why doesn't the sea flood all over the land?
Because it's tide.

What washes up on very small beaches?
Microwaves.

What did one rock pool say to the other rock pool?
'Show us your mussels.'

Why is the sea suspicious?
Because it's been crossed so often.

How do you cut the ocean in half?
With a sea-saw.

What did Neptune say when the sea dried up?
'I haven't a notion.'

What is the difference between an iceberg and a clothes brush?
One crushes boats and the other brushes coats.

*See also **Fish**; **Sailors**; **Ships**.*

Sex

'I believe sex between two people is a beautiful experience. Between five it's fantastic!' *(Woody Allen)*

Sex isn't the answer. Sex is the question. Yes is the answer.

Parishioner Do you believe in sex before marriage, vicar?
Vicar Not if it delays the service.

The vicar never entertained lewd thoughts. They entertained him.

'Have you heard the one about the retired general who said he had not had sex since 1956? His friend said, "That's a long time ago." "I don't know," the general replied, "it's only 20.27 now." ' *(Ronnie Barker)*

Wife What do you like most in me, my pretty face or my sexy body?
Husband Your sense of humour.

'Of course I believe in safe sex. I've got a handrail around the bed.' *(Ken Dodd)*

'He had ambitions at one time to become a sex maniac, but he failed his practical.' *(Les Dawson)*

'I recently sold the rights of my love life to Parker brothers, they're going to turn it into a game.' *(Woody Allen)*

See also **Dating**; **Love**.

Sharks

What did the shark say on handing a poorly octopus to his friend the jellyfish?
'Here's that six quid I owe you.'

Where do sharks go on holiday?
Finland.

What do you get from a man-eating shark?
As far away as possible.

Two fishermen are sitting with their legs in the water when a shark swims up and bites one man's leg off. 'A shark's bitten my leg off!' the man screams. 'Which one?' asks the other. 'How should I know – they all look the same to me!'

There was a young lady from Guam
Who said, 'Now the ocean's so calm
I will swim, for a lark.'
She encountered a shark.
Let us now sing the ninetieth psalm.

See also **Fish**.

Sheep

How do sheep stay warm?
Central bleating.

What do sheep like on hot days?
Baabaacues.

What do you call a sheep with no legs?
A cloud.

Why are sheep always short of money?
They keep getting fleeced.

Where do sheep get their hair cut?
At the baaber's.

What do polite sheep say?
'After ewe.'

Why did the ram run over the cliff?
He didn't see the ewe turn.

Why did Bo Peep lose her sheep?
She had a crook with her.

What do you get if you cross a dog with a sheep?
A sheep that rounds itself up.

What do you get if you cross a sheep with a rainstorm?
A wet blanket.

Shellfish

Which shellfish is the strongest?
The muscle.

Where do shellfish go to borrow money?
To the prawn broker.

Why did the lobster blush?
It saw the *Queen Mary*'s bottom.

Why don't lobsters share?
They're shellfish.

Why did the lobster blush?
It saw the salad dressing.

What do you get if you cross a shellfish with a camera?
A clamera.

See also **Crabs**.

Ships

How can you tell if a ship is in love with the land?
It hugs the shore.

What lies at the bottom of the sea and shivers?
A nervous wreck.

What does a houseboat become when it grows up?
A township.

A boat set sail with 99 passengers. When it capsized and turned over, how many passengers were there?
66.

What kind of ship never sinks?
Friendship.

Did you hear about the ship that sank in a lake full of piranhas?
It returned with a skeleton crew.

What do you get if you cross the Atlantic with the *Titanic*?
About halfway.

See also **Sailors**; **Sea**.

Shoes

A small boy complains to his mother that his new trainers hurt. 'You've got them on the wrong feet, darling,' says his mother. 'But these are the only feet I have!'

There once was a man from Peru
Who dreamed he was eating his shoe.
He awoke with a fright
In the middle of the night
And found that his dream had come true.

'Knock, knock.'
'Who's there?'
'Juicy.'
'Juicy who?'
'Juicy my shoes anywhere?'

Why don't bears wear shoes?
They prefer bear feet.

Which animal goes to sleep with its shoes on?
A horse.

What two kinds of fish do you need to make a shoe?
A sole and an eel.

What do ghosts wear in wet weather?
Boo-oots and ghouloshes.

Shopping

A man goes into a newsagent's and asks, 'Do you keep stationery here?' 'No,' replies the sales assistant, 'sometimes I move about a bit.'

The Church of England are going to open a chain of supermarkets. They are calling them Jesus Christ Superstores.

A duck walks into a chemist's and buys some lipstick. She then goes to the counter and tells the sales assistant, 'Just put it on my bill.'

When you've seen one shopping centre you've seen a mall.

Where do cats do their shopping?
In catalogues.

My wife went window-shopping the other day. She bought six windows.

'I had my credit card stolen, but I didn't report it because the thief was spending less than my wife did.' *(Henny Youngman)*

Sickness *See Doctors; Hospitals; Ill-health.*

Skeletons

What do you call a skeleton who stays in bed in the morning?
Lazybones.

What do you call a lazy skeleton?
Bone idle.

What do skeletons say before they eat?
'Bone appetit.'

What did the skeleton order for dinner?
Spare ribs.

What vegetable do skeletons like best?
Marrow.

What do skeletons eat off?
Bone china.

A skeleton walks into a bar and tells the barman, 'Give me a beer and a mop.'

Why did the skeleton go to the library?
He wanted to bone up on his studies.

Why did the skeleton go to the party?
To have a rattling good time.

What musical instrument do skeletons like to play?
The trombone.

Why don't skeletons play music in church?
They have no organs.

Why did the skeleton lie on a sunbed?
To get a skeletan.

Why do skeletons hate winter?
The wind goes right through them.

What do you call a skeleton who goes out in the snow
with no hat?
A numbskull.

Why did the one-handed skeleton cross the road?
To get to the second-hand shop.

Why didn't the skeleton cross the road?
He didn't have the guts.

See also **Ghosts**.

Skunks

What has a bad smell and flies?
A dead skunk.

What do you call a dead skunk?
Exstinkt.

What do you call a flying skunk?
A smellicopter.

What do you get if you cross a bear and a skunk?
Winnie-the-Pooh.

What do you get if you cross an eagle with a skunk?
A bird that stinks to high heaven.

What do you get if you cross a skunk with an owl?
A bird that smells but doesn't give a hoot.

What do you get if you cross a dog and a skunk?
Rid of the dog.

Skydiving See *Extreme sports*.

Sleep

Why did the boy sprinkle sugar on his pillow before he
went to sleep?
So he could have sweet dreams.

Did you hear about the man who dreamed he was eating a
giant marshmallow?
When he woke up he couldn't find his pillow.

What does a cat sleep on?
A caterpillow.

Why isn't it safe to sleep on trains?
Because they run over sleepers.

Have you heard about the new corduroy pillows?
They're making headlines.

What's the difference between a butcher and a light sleeper?
One weighs a steak and the other stays awake.

Why did the man run around his bed?
He wanted to catch up with his sleep.

'I haven't slept for days.'
'Why not?'
'I sleep at night.'

'Doctor, doctor, I can't get to sleep!'
'Lie on the edge of the bed and you'll soon drop off.'

Why did the nurse tiptoe past the medicine cabinet?
She didn't want to wake the sleeping pills.

What do you give an elephant with insomnia?
Trunkquillizers.

Why did the elephant sleep in a bowl of salad dressing?
So he'd wake up really oily.

What did the blanket say to the bed?
'I've got you covered.'

'Why are you looking in the mirror with your eyes closed?'
'I want to know what I look like when I'm asleep.'

There was an old man of Calcutta
Who coated his tonsils with butter,
Thus converting his snore
From a thunderous roar
To a soft, oleaginous mutter.

'Doctor, doctor, I snore so loudly I can't sleep properly!'
'Sleep in another room, then.'

What has a bed but does not sleep?
A river.

What kind of bed does a mermaid sleep in?
A water bed.

Who sleeps at the bottom of the sea?
Jack the kipper.

What do you call a sleep-walking nun?
A roamin' Catholic.

Slugs and snails

What sort of animal is a slug?
A snail with a housing problem.

What is a snail?
A slug with a crash helmet.

Two slugs turn a corner on a path and find themselves
stuck behind two snails. 'Oh, no,' says one slug to the
other, 'caravans!'

Why is a snail stronger than an elephant?
A snail can carry its house on its back.

How do snails get their shells so shiny?
Snail varnish.

Where do you find giant snails?
At the end of a giant's fingers.

What should you do if two snails have a fight?
Leave them to slug it out.

What was the snail doing on the motorway?
Less than one mile a day.

A snail enters a restaurant one Friday night and asks for a table for one. The waiter picks him up in disgust and throws him out of the door and across the road. The following Friday the snail comes back through the door, catches his breath and says, 'What did you do that for?'

A snail is crossing the road when it is run over by a turtle. The unconscious snail is rushed to hospital and is on life support for several days before eventually recovering. The doctors ask him what happened, but the snail can only shake its head: 'I don't know, it all happened so fast!'

Smells

'My dog's got no nose.'
'How does he smell, then?'
'Terrible.'

How do you stop a dog smelling?
Hold its nose.

How many wet Labradors does it take to stink a house out?
Quite a phew.

What's black and smelly and hangs from the ceiling?
A bad electrician.

What's the smelliest city in the USA?
Phew York.

What's brown, smelly and sounds like a bell?
Dung.

What lies on the ground 100 feet up in the air and smells?
A dead centipede.

'Doctor, doctor, my husband smells like a fish!'
'Poor sole.'

See also **Skunks**.

Smoking

What did the big chimney say to the little chimney?
'You're too young to smoke.'

Did you hear about the man who was shocked when he
read about the dangers of smoking?
He gave up reading.

There was a young fellow named Vivian
Who had a dear friend, a Bolivian,
Who dropped his cigar
In a gunpowder jar –
His spirit is now in oblivion.

'I've taken up smoking. My doctor says I'm not getting
enough tar in my diet.' *(Steve Martin)*

See also **Ill-health**.

Snails See **Slugs and snails**.

Snakes

Which hand should you use to handle a poisonous snake?
Someone else's.

Rabbits multiply, but only snakes can be adders.

What's green and slimy and goes 'hith'?
A snake with a lisp.

What do you call a nest of snakes?
Mass hissteria.

How do snakes sign their letters?
With love and hisses.

What do you get if you cross a snake with a bird?
A feather boa.

What do you get if you cross a bag of snakes with a
cupboard of food?
Snakes and larders.

Snowmen

What do snowmen eat for breakfast?
Snowflakes.

What do you call a snowman in the desert?
A puddle.

Where do snowmen go to dance?
A snowball.

Where do snowmen keep their money?
In snow banks.

What do you call a snowman on roller blades?
A snow mobile.

What do you get if you cross a snowman with a vampire?
Frostbite.

Soccer See **Football**.

Soldiers

'How long was I in the army? Five foot eleven.' *(Spike Milligan)*

'Knock, knock.'
'Who's there?'
'Major.'
'Major who?'
'Major answer, didn't I?'

Why do guardsmen keep catching colds?
They go about in their bearskins.

What do you call a rifle with three barrels?
A trifle.

Did you hear about the karate expert who joined the army?
The first time he saluted he killed himself.

Two soldiers are having lunch when one of them asks the other to pass him the cake. 'I can't, I'm afraid,' says the second man. 'It's against regulations to help another soldier to dessert.'

A corporal orders a private to mend the fence round an army camp. 'You'll need some planks, a box of nails and a namafor.' 'What's a namafor?' asks the private. 'For banging the nails in, idiot!'

Three soldiers face a firing squad. As the men take aim the first soldier shouts, 'Avalanche!' and, as the men look away, runs off. When the men take aim again the second soldier shouts, 'Flood!' and, as the men look away, also runs off. The third soldier waits until the men take aim a third time, grins and shouts, 'Fire!'

'I was classified "4P" by the draftboard. In the event of war, I'm a hostage.' *(Woody Allen)*

Space

What did one shooting star say to the other?
'Pleased to meteor.'

What is heavier, a full moon or a half moon?
A half moon, because a full moon is lighter.

Why are the man in the moon's parties always a failure?
There's just no atmosphere.

What keeps the sun up in the sky?
Sunbeams.

Why were the stupid astronauts so sure they could land on the sun without being burned to death?
They were going to land at night.

*See also **Aliens**; **Astronauts**.*

Spelling

Supercalifragilisticexpialidocious. How do you spell it?
I T.

I saw Esau sitting on a see-saw. How many Ss in that?
There aren't any in 'that'.

What always comes at the end of everything?
G.

What starts with a P, ends with an E and has millions of letters in it?
Post Office.

What happens if you take the pee out of a pirate?
He becomes irate.

What starts with an E and ends with an E but has only one letter in it?
Envelope.

How do you get rid of varnish?
Drop the R and make it vanish.

Why is Alabama the smartest state in the USA?
Because it has four As and one B.

What is the longest word of all?
Smiles, because there's a mile between the beginning and the end.

When his wife dies, a Yorkshireman orders a stonemason to carve a headstone for her grave with the words 'She Was Thine'. When the headstone is finished, however, he sees that the man has made a mistake and that the stone reads 'She Was Thin'. The widower points out the mistake and insists that the missing E be restored. Convinced the problem will soon be sorted out he leaves the stonemason to his work. The next time he checks the gravestone it reads 'E, She Was Thin'.

There once was a writer named Wright
Who instructed his son to write right;
He said, 'Son, write Wright right.
It is not right to write
Wright as "rite" – try to write Wright aright!'

See also **Alphabet**.

Spiders

Why did the spider buy a car?
So he could take it out for a spin.

How do spiders travel long distances?
They use the worldwide web.

What do French spiders like to eat?
French flies.

What do you call a big Irish spider?
Paddy long legs.

What does a spider do when he gets angry?
He goes up the wall.

Spitting *See* **Manners**.

Sports

You have a referee in football and an umpire in cricket,
but what do you have in bowls?
Goldfish.

'I was watching the Indy 500. I was thinking that if they
left earlier they wouldn't have to go so fast.' *(Steven
Wright)*

What has eleven heads and runs around screaming?
A girls' hockey team.

Did you hear what happened to the ice hockey team when
they went out for spring training?
They drowned.

Did you hear about the stupid cyclist who won the Tour
de France?
He did a lap of honour.

How many people can you get into an empty sports
stadium?
One. After that it's no longer empty.

What sport do elephants most enjoy?
Squash.

See also **Athletics**; **Boxing**; **Cricket**; **Extreme sports**;
Fishing; **Football**; **Swimming**.

Stamps *See* **Letters**.

Stupidity

Did you hear about the stupid ghost?
He climbed over walls.

Why did the stupid chicken climb over the glass wall?
To see what was on the other side.

'You're stupid!'
'How dare you! Say you're sorry!'
'All right, I'm sorry you're stupid!'

'Why, a child of four could understand this report. Run
outside and get me a child of four. I can't make head or
tail of it.' *(Groucho Marx)*

'This match won't light!'
'That's funny. It did this morning.'

A roadworker is told to dig a hole in the road. 'What shall
I do with the soil?' he asks his boss. 'Don't be stupid,' says
his boss. 'Dig another hole and bury it.'

Did you hear about the stupid Kamikaze pilot?
He flew fifty-seven missions.

'What's the difference between ignorance and apathy?'
'I don't know and I don't care.'

See also **Dumb blondes**; **Idiots**.

Success

There are two rules for success in life. One is never tell
everything you know.

Why are astronauts successful people?
Because they always go up in the world.

Where does success come before work?
In the dictionary.

Why is a successful businessman like a bad waiter?
They both have a finger in many pies.

Suicide

Did you hear about the ice-cream man who was found
lying on the floor of his van covered with chocolate sauce
and hundreds and thousands?
Police say that he topped himself.

Did you hear about the man who tried to kill himself by
swallowing a whole bottle of aspirins?
After he had taken two he felt much better.

Did you hear about the blonde suicide bomber?
She dyed by her own hand.

An inmate in a lunatic asylum prevents another inmate from drowning himself. Duly impressed by the man's responsible behaviour, the doctors review the man's case with a view to releasing him back into the community. 'We are only sorry,' they tell him, 'that the man you saved later tied a rope round his neck and hanged himself.' 'Oh,' replies the hero, 'he didn't hang himself. I hung him up to dry.'

See also **Death**.

Swimming

'Where did you learn to swim?'
'In the water.'

A man is about to dive off the diving board into an empty pool. 'Stop!' shouts the lifeguard. 'There's no water in there!' 'That's all right,' the man replies, 'I can't swim!'

'Why do you keep swimming the backstroke?'
'I haven't had lunch yet and I don't want to swim on an empty stomach.'

What food is dangerous to swimmers?
Currants.

'So I rang up my local swimming baths. I said, "Is that the local swimming baths?" He said, "It depends where you're calling from." ' *(Tim Vine)*

Why were the elephants thrown out of the swimming pool?
They kept dropping their trunks.

An English cat called One, Two, Three and a French cat called Un, Deux, Trois decide to have a swimming race across the Channel. Only the English cat makes it to the other side. Why?
Because Un, Deux, Trois, Quatre Cinq.

T

Taxation

Newsflash: There has been a fire at the local tax office, but it was put out before any serious good could be done.

Why don't sharks attack tax inspectors?
Professional courtesy.

A circus strongman offers a prize of £1,000 to anyone who can prove they are stronger than him. To win the money a challenger has to watch while the strongman uses all his strength to squeeze the juice out of a lemon. If the challenger can then squeeze out one more drop he will be declared the winner. Challenger after challenger attempts the feat but such is the strongman's strength that no one succeeds. Eventually, a puny little man struggles to the front of the crowd and says he would like to try. When the laughter has died down the strongman squeezes the lemon dry and hands it to him. 'Go on then, squirt, let's see you try!' The puny little man closes his fist round the lemon and squeezes. To everyone's amazement three large drops of juice fall from the fruit. The crowd cheers and the circus bosses hand over the prize of £1,000. 'What do you do for a living?' asks the stunned strongman. 'Are you a weightlifter or something?' 'Oh, no,' says the puny little man, 'I'm just a taxman.'

If a lawyer and a taxman were both drowning and you could save just one, would you read the paper or go to lunch?

See also **Business**.

Teachers

Where are teachers made?
On an assembly line.

Why do teachers wear sunglasses?
Because their pupils are so bright.

Why was the cross-eyed teacher sacked?
He couldn't control his pupils.

Why did the one-eyed headteacher have to close his school?
He had only one pupil.

Why did the teacher jump into the lake?
She wanted to test the waters.

Did you hear about the maths teacher who fainted in class?
Everyone tried to bring her two.

Why did the maths teacher take a ruler to bed with him?
To see how long he would sleep.

What's the difference between a teacher and a railway guard?
One trains the mind and the other minds the train.

What is the difference between a teacher and a train?
A teacher says, 'Stop chewing that sweet!' A train says,
'Choo, choo!'

'My teacher's a peach.'
'Is she sweet?'
'No, she has a heart of stone.'

What's the difference between a mean teacher and a crazy
dog?
One marks badly and the other barks madly.

What is the difference between a boring teacher and a
boring book?
You can shut the book up.

What meals do maths teachers like to eat?
Take aways.

What do maths teachers like for dessert?
Pi.

What do history teachers have when they go out together?
Dates.

Why did the art teacher fall ill?
She had pencilitis.

In the old days a teacher named Bind
Gave my dad, in manner unkind,
Heavy whacks to the head
With a flat piece of lead,
Saying, 'This lesson will broaden your mind.'

What do you get if you cross a teacher with a vampire?
Blood tests.

Did you hear about the ghost teachers who went on strike?
They were replaced by a skeleton staff.

Teacher Every time I turn round I find you doing something you shouldn't be doing. What are we going to do about that?
Pupil How about you tell me when you're going to turn round?

Martin Teacher likes me better than you.
Gregory How do you know?
Martin She puts more kisses in my book than she does in yours.

'I don't want to go to school today, Mummy. The teachers all think I'm stupid and the kids all hate me!'
'Now come along, darling, you have to go. You're the headmaster.'

See also **Higher education**; **School**.

Technology *See* **Computers**; **Telephones**; **Television**.

Teddy bears

What was the bald teddy bear called?
Fred Bear.

What did the teddy bear say when he was offered seconds?
'No, thanks, I'm stuffed.'

How do you start a teddy bear race?
'Ready, teddy, go!'

What do you get if you cross a teddy bear with a pig?
A teddy boar.

What do you get if you cross a bear with a freezer?
A teddy brrrr.

See also **Bears**.

Teeth

'My teeth are like stars.'
'Yes, they come out at night!'

Which two letters are bad for your teeth?
D K.

There once was a walrus named Lou
Who lived in a place called the zoo.
He said to his friend,
'Do my teeth ever end?
I can't see past them, can you?'

What did one tooth say to the other tooth?
'Get your cap on, the dentist is taking us out tonight.'

What has teeth but cannot eat?
A comb.

What's red and bad for your teeth?
A brick.

'Knock, knock.'
'Who's there?'
'Dishes.'
'Dishes who?'
'Dishes the way I talk with my new false teeth.'

What's grey, has a wand, huge wings and gives money to elephants?
The tusk fairy.

See also **Dentists**.

Telephones

What did the big telephone say to the little telephone?
'You're too young to be engaged.'

What do angels say when they answer the phone?
'Halo.'

How do telephones get married?
They exchange rings.

What do you get if you cross a dog with a telephone?
A golden receiver.

'So I got home, and the phone was ringing. I picked it up, and said, "Who's speaking, please?" And a voice said, "You are." ' *(Tim Vine)*

Television

What do birds watch on television?
The feather forecast.

What television programme do cats watch?
The evening mews.

Two aerials met on a roof and fell in love. The wedding
was nothing special but the reception was fantastic.

What illness did the crew of the *Enterprise* catch?
Chicken Spocks.

'I find television very educating. Every time someone
turns on the set I go into the other room and read a book.'
(Groucho Marx)

Theatre See **Acting**.

Tigers

Why do tigers have stripes?
Because they don't want to be spotted.

What do you get a bad-tempered tiger for his birthday?
I don't know, but you'd better hope he likes it.

What steps should you take if a man-eating tiger comes
into the room?
Very long ones.

There was a young lady from Riga
Who rode with a smile on a tiger.
They returned from the ride
With the lady inside,
And the smile on the face of the tiger.

'Have you ever seen a man-eating tiger?'
'No, but I have seen a man eating chicken.'

A vicar visits the zoo and accidentally falls into the tiger's enclosure. Seeing a hungry-looking tiger approaching him, the vicar puts his hands together to pray. To his surprise, the tiger does the same thing. 'This is a miracle!' breathes the vicar. 'I thought you were going to eat me but instead you're saying your prayers!' 'Shut up,' says the tiger, 'I'm saying grace.'

What do you get if you cross a tiger with a kangaroo?
A stripy jumper.

Time

What is always behind time?
The back of a clock.

What occurs once in a minute, twice in a moment but never in a day?
The letter M.

Why did the pupil walk backwards on the first day of school?
He was told it was back to school time.

What is procrastination?
I'll tell you tomorrow.

'Why should I care about posterity? What has posterity ever done for me?' *(Groucho Marx)*

*See also **Calendars**; **Clocks and watches**.*

Toads *See Frogs and toads*.

Toilets

What is the difference between a person who needs the toilet and a person who is very ill?
One is dying to go and the other is going to die.

Which French town has two toilets?
Toulouse.

What do you call a flag flying over a toilet?
Bog-standard.

Why did the doctor keep his wife under the bed?
He thought she was a little potty.

'The toilets at a local police station have been stolen.
Police say they have nothing to go on.' *(Ronnie Barker)*

Tortoises

Where would you find a tortoise with no legs?
Where you left it.

Why was the tortoise shy?
It wouldn't come out of its shell.

Did you hear what happened when a lorryload of tortoises crashed into a lorryload of terrapins?
It was a turtle disaster.

Why did the homeless tortoise cross the road?
To get to the Shell garage.

Traffic wardens

Why do traffic wardens have yellow bands round their
hats?
To stop people parking on their heads.

What do traffic wardens put on their sandwiches?
Traffic jam.

What do you call a traffic warden who never gives out
parking tickets?
A triffic warden.

Somebody complimented me on my driving today. They
left a little note on the windscreen saying, 'Parking Fine.'
So that was nice.

See also **Cars**; **Motorists**; **Police officers**.

Travel

Did you hear about the man who ate a whole pack of
travel sweets?
He was really cross when he didn't go anywhere.

A man and his wife are on holiday, when the wife
suddenly gasps in alarm. 'I just remembered I left the oven
on! The house will catch fire.' 'Don't worry,' replies her
husband, 'I just remembered I left the tap running.'

A tourist visits London and is impressed by the size of the London Eye. 'It's enormous!' he cries. A Londoner hears him and agrees, 'Yes, and you should see the hamster!'

A tourist from Texas is being taken on a tour by taxi round the sights of London. 'What's that building?' he asks the driver. 'The Tower of London, sir.' 'Heck, we could put up something like that in two weeks back in Texas.' A few minutes later he interrupts the driver again. 'What's that building?' he demands. 'That's Buckingham Palace, sir.' 'Shucks, we could put up one of those in a week.' Next comes Westminster Abbey. 'And what's that building there?' the American asks. 'Sorry, sir, I've no idea,' replies the taxi driver. 'It wasn't there this morning!'

See also **Astronauts**; **Aviation**; **Cars**; **Holidays**; **Motorists**; **Rail travel**; **Ships**.

Trees

What kind of tree can you wear?
A fir.

What kind of tree fits in your hand?
A palm.

What kind of trees are the most diseased?
Sycamores.

Why did the tree dye its hair?
Its roots were showing.

What did the pine tree say to his girlfriend?
'I'm fir you.'

What kind of trees do plumbers like?
Toiletries.

What did the beaver say to the tree?
'It's been good gnawing you.'

U

Ugliness

I knew a woman who had a baby that was so ugly she didn't push the pram, she pulled it!

'I was so ugly when I was born the doctor slapped my mother.' *(Henny Youngman)*

'Some boys say I'm pretty. Some boys say I'm ugly. What do you say?'
'I say both. Pretty ugly.'

'I never forget a face, but in your case I'll make an exception.' *(Groucho Marx)*

'Will you love me when I'm old and ugly?'
'Darling, of course I do.'

'Marry me and I'll never look at another horse!' *(Groucho Marx)*

Two women are at a party when one suddenly exclaims, 'Look at that man over there! Have you ever seen anyone so hideously ugly?' 'That is my husband,' the other woman replies frostily. 'I'm so sorry!' the first woman blurts in embarrassment. To which the other replies, '*You're* sorry . . . !'

'You know, I could rent you out as a decoy for duck hunters.' *(Groucho Marx)*

'You have the face of a saint!'
'Do I?'
'Yes, Saint Bernard.'

'You look like a million dollars!'
'Thanks.'
'All green and wrinkly.'

Undertakers

Do undertakers enjoy their work?
Of corpse they do.

Why did the undertaker chop all the bodies into bits?
So they could rest in pieces.

What did the undertaker say to his girlfriend?
'Em-balmy about you.'

Where do undertakers go in October?
The hearse of the year show.

See also **Death**; **Funerals**.

Underwear

What goes 'pant . . . pant'?
A pair of pants.

'Knock, knock.'
'Who's there?'
'Nicholas.'
'Nicholas who?'
'Nicholas girls shouldn't climb trees!'

What flies down a washing line at 100 miles per hour?
Hondapants.

A vest is something a boy wears when his mother feels cold.

What do Australians wear under their trousers?
Down underwear.

See also **Clothing**.

V

Vacations *See **Holidays**.*

Vampires

What are twin vampires called?
Blood brothers.

Why do you never get fat vampires?
Because they eat necks to nothing.

What do vampires do between feeds?
They have a coffin break.

What are vampires' favourite fruits?
Blood oranges and necktarines.

What do vampires enjoy for dessert?
Veinilla ice cream.

Why did the vampire bite Indiana Jones?
He had a taste for adventure.

Where did the vampire bite the clown?
In his juggler vein.

What do vampires call a person with high blood pressure?
Fast food.

What do polite vampires say?
'Fang you very much.'

Why did the vampire go to the blood bank?
He wanted to make a withdrawal.

Which animal do vampires like best?
Giraffes.

Which dance do vampires like best?
The fang-dango.

What do vampires sing on New Year's Eve?
Auld Fang Syne.

With whom did the vampire fall in love?
The girl necks door.

What kind of mail does a vampire get?
Fang mail.

Why did the vampire have no friends?
He was a pain in the neck.

Which public holiday do American vampires celebrate?
Fangsgiving.

Why did the vampire have a second career as an artist?
He was great at drawing blood.

How do vampires cross the sea?
They go in blood vessels.

What happened to the mad vampire?
He went batty.

What's the difference between a vampire with toothache and a rainstorm?
One roars with pain while the other pours with rain.

What did the vampire call his new false teeth?
A new-fangled device.

Two nuns are driving along a lonely road when a vampire suddenly lands on the bonnet of their car. 'Quick,' screams one of the nuns. 'Show it your cross!' So the other nun leans out of the window and shouts, 'Oi! You! Get lost!'

Why did the vampire drive a stake into his own chest?
He was a man after his own heart.

What kind of coffee does Dracula drink?
Decoffinated.

Who was Dracula in love with?
His girlfiend.

Where does Dracula buy his pencils?
Pencilvania.

What is Dracula's favourite dinner?
The quiche of death.

What is Dracula's favourite pudding?
Leeches and cream.

What is Dracula's favourite sport?
Batminton.

Where does Dracula stay when he visits the USA?
The Vampire State Building.

Where does Dracula keep his savings?
In a blood bank.

Vegetables

Did you hear about the carrot that got hit by a car?
He's going to be a vegetable for the rest of his life.

Why should you never share a secret in a field?
Because corn has ears, potatoes have eyes and beanstalk.

Why did the corn get cross with the farmer?
Because he kept pulling its ears.

There was a young lady named Perkins
Who just simply doted on gherkins.
In spite of advice,
She ate so much spice
That she pickled her internal workin's.

What vegetable do plumbers like best?
Leeks.

Which vegetables are found in toilets?
Leeks and peas.

There was a young lady from Jarrow
Whose mouth was exceedingly narrow;
She ate with a spoon
By the light of the moon,
But all she could eat was a marrow.

What is a mushroom?
Where they keep the school food.

Why did the mushroom buy a round of drinks?
Because he was a fungi.

Which is the most unreliable vegetable?
A fickle onion.

What has eyes but cannot see?
A potato.

What did they call the potato who insulted the farmer?
A fresh vegetable.

Why did the farmer drive a steamroller through his potato field?
He wanted to grow mashed potatoes.

What is the fastest vegetable of them all?
A runner bean.

What's green and white and bounces?
A spring onion.

What's the difference between a bogey and a sprout?
Kids won't eat sprouts.

What do you get if you cross a door-knocker with some tomatoes, onions, courgettes and garlic?
Rat-a-tat-a-touille.

How do you attract a vegetarian?
Make a noise like a wounded vegetable.

*See also **Food**; **Fruit***.

Vegetarians See *Vegetables*.

Vets

What qualification do you need to become a vet?
A pedigree.

How do vets make sick birds better?
They give them tweetment.

A man arrives at the vet's to collect his sick dog. The vet carries the dog into the room and says, 'I'm sorry, but I'm going to have to put your dog down.' The man bursts into tears. 'Why?' 'Because he's too heavy.'

A man takes his sick hamster to the vet's, but after a brief examination the vet tells him the animal is dead. 'He can't be!' says the man. 'I want a second opinion.' The vet sighs, then opens the door and lets a cat into the surgery. The cat inspects the hamster then utters a single 'Miaow' and goes out again. 'The cat says it's dead too,' says the vet. 'I insist upon another opinion!' says the man. The vet goes out of the room and comes back with a Labrador. The Labrador examines the hamster and after a moment utters a single bark and then leaves the room. 'The Labrador says it's dead as well.' The man finally accepts the vet's opinion and says he will pay the bill. He is shocked, however, when he is handed a bill for £500. 'I didn't think it would be so much!' says the man. 'Well,' says the vet, 'it's £50 for my opinion, but then there's £150 for the cat scan and £300 for the lab work.'

See also **Animals**.

Vicars

What did they call the motorbike-riding vicar?
Rev.

What did the vicar say when he was told that the church was on fire?
'Holy smoke!'

How do vicars keep in touch over the telephone?
They make parson-to-parson calls.

A vicar is walking down the street when a young woman slips on the pavement in front of him. The vicar helps her up, joking, 'This is the first time I've rescued a fallen woman.' The woman replies, 'And this is the first time I've been picked up by a clergyman.'

A vicar retires after twenty years in his parish. 'We're sorry you're retiring,' says one parishioner, 'you showed us what sin really is.'

There once was a pious young priest
Who lived almost wholly on yeast;
He said, 'For it's plain
We must all rise again
And I wanted to get started, at least.'

See also **Religion**.

Visitors *See* *Callers*.

Volcanoes

What is a volcano?
A mountain with hiccups.

What do you call an extinct volcano?
A blast from the past.

What did the first volcano say to the second volcano?
'Do you lava me like I lava you?'

'My wife had an accident on a volcano.'
'Krakatoa?'
'No. She broke her leg.'

See also **Earthquakes**.

Waiter, waiter

'Waiter, waiter, is there soup on the menu?'
'No, sir, I wiped it off.'

'Waiter, waiter, there's a fly in my soup!'
'Don't worry, sir, it's not hot enough to burn him.'

'Waiter, waiter, what's this fly doing in my soup?'
'Looks like the breaststroke, sir.'

'Waiter, waiter, what do you call this?'
'That's bean soup, sir.'
'I don't care what it's been – what is it now?'

'Waiter, waiter, your thumb is in my soup!'
'It's all right, madam, it's not hot.'

'Waiter, waiter, there's a fly in my bread!'
'Don't worry, sir, the spider in the butter will catch it.'

'Waiter, waiter, bring me something to eat, and make it snappy.'
'How about a crocodile sandwich, sir?'

'Waiter, waiter, there's a hair in my sandwich!'
'Don't shout, sir, or everyone will want one.'

'Waiter, waiter, this lobster's only got one claw.'
'It was probably in a fight, sir.'
'Well, bring me the winner!'

'Waiter, waiter, there's a fly in my salad.'
'I'm sorry, sir, I didn't know you were a vegetarian.'

'Waiter, waiter, there's a small slug in my lettuce!'
'Sorry, madam, shall I get you a larger one?'

'Waiter, waiter, there's a button in my lettuce!'
'Oh, that must be from the salad dressing.'

'Waiter, waiter, this food isn't fit for a pig!'
'One moment, sir, and I'll bring you some that is.'

'Waiter, waiter, do you have frogs' legs?'
'No, madam, I just walk this way.'

'Waiter, waiter, you've brought me the wrong order!'
'Well, you did say you wanted something different.'

'Waiter, waiter, take your thumb off my steak!'
'You don't want me to drop it again, do you?'

'Waiter, waiter, bring me a glass of milk and a Dover sole.'
'Fillet?'
'Yes, to the brim.'

'Waiter, waiter, what's wrong with this fish?'
'Long time, no sea.'

'Waiter, waiter, I've just swallowed a fish bone!'
'Are you choking?'
'No, I'm totally serious!'

'Waiter, waiter, will my pizza be long?'
'No, sir, round.'

'Waiter, waiter, how long will my sausages be?'
'About three inches.'

'Waiter, waiter, there's a fly in my wine!'
'You did ask for something with a little body in it, sir.'

'Waiter, waiter, I don't like cheese with holes.'
'Well, leave the holes at the side of your plate.'

'Waiter, waiter, this coffee tastes like earth.'
'Well, sir, it was ground yesterday.'

'Waiter, waiter, bring me some tea without milk.'
'We haven't any milk. Will tea without cream do instead?'

'Waiter, waiter, how long have you been here?'
'Six months.'
'Ah, well, it can't have been you who took my order.'

War See **Soldiers**.

Watches See **Clocks and watches**.

Weather

What should you do if it rains cats and dogs?
Take care not to stand in a poodle.

What's worse than raining cats and dogs?
Hailing taxis.

What did the puddle say to the rain?
'Drop in sometime.'

What did the cloud say to the other cloud?
'I'm cirrus about you.'

Why is lightning badly behaved?
It doesn't know how to conduct itself.

What do clouds wear under their clothes?
Thunderwear.

What goes in pink and comes out blue?
A swimmer in cold weather.

Why is it more difficult to keep a secret when the weather's cold?
Because your teeth chatter.

Did you hear about the dumb blonde who went outside with only one glove on?
She had heard that it might be warm, but on the other hand it might be cool.

Why do people who get sunburn have only themselves to blame?
Because they are getting what they basked for.

Why did the weather forecaster lose his job overseas?
The climate didn't agree with him.

Weddings See *Marriage*.

Werewolves

What kind of fur do you get from a werewolf?
As fur away as you can.

Who are the werewolves' cousins?
The whatwolves and the whenwolves.

Why did the boy take a painkiller after hearing the
werewolf howl?
Because it gave him eerie ache.

What do you get if you cross a werewolf with a sculptor?
Hairy Potter.

I used to be a werewolf but I'm all right noooooooow . . .

See also **Wolves**.

Whales

What does Moby Dick do on his birthday?
He has a whale of a time.

Where do whales go to get themselves weighed?
The whale weigh station.

What do you call a baby whale that never stops crying?
A little blubber.

What do you get if you cross a whale with a computer?
A four-ton know it all.

See also **Fish**.

Wind See *Manners*.

Witches

How does a witch tell the time?
She looks at her witch watch.

What kind of jewellery do witches wear on their wrists?
Charm bracelets.

What do you call two witches sharing a room?
Broom-mates.

What do you call a witch who inspects the activities of her coven?
A spell checker.

What do you call a nervous witch?
A twitch.

Why is a witch like a candle?
They are both wicked.

What do you call a witch who drives really badly?
A road hag.

Why do witches get good bargains?
They like to haggle.

Who turns the lights off at Halloween?
The light's witch.

What do witches put on their hair?
Scarespray.

What happens to witches who don't do their homework?
They get ex-spelled.

Why did the witch stop telling fortunes?
She couldn't see any future in it.

How do you make a witch scratch?
Drop the W to make her itch.

What do you get if you cross a sorceress with a
millionaire?
A very witch person.

What do you get if you cross a witch with an iceberg?
A cold spell.

Why do witches fly on broomsticks?
Because vacuum cleaners don't have long enough cords.

What happens to a witch if she loses her temper while
riding her broom?
She flies off the handle.

What goes 'moorb, moorb'?
A witch flying backwards.

What do you get if you cross a broomstick with a
motorbike?
A broom, broom, broomstick.

What do you get if you cross a witch with an ice cube?
A cold spell.

'Doctor, doctor, I think I'm a witch!'
'Lie down for a spell.'

What was the name of the witch's father?
He was cauldron.

What did the wizard say to his witch girlfriend?
'Hello, gore-juice.'

What do wizards stop for on the motorway?
Witchhikers.

Did you hear about the wizard who brushed his teeth with gunpowder?
He kept shooting his mouth off.

What do you call a wizard from outer space?
A flying sorcerer.

Wolves

What sort of animals are made of wood?
Timber wolves.

Why are wolves like playing cards?
They both come in packs.

What happened when the wolf fell into the washing machine?
He became a wash and werewolf.

A pack of wolves are chasing two rabbits, which take refuge in a thorn bush. The wolves prowl around, waiting for the rabbits to make their move. One rabbit turns to the other and says, 'What do you want to do – make a break for it or stay here a few days until we outnumber them?'

See also **Werewolves**.

Women

God made man and then rested. God made woman and then no one rested.

There are three types of women: the intelligent, the beautiful and the majority.

Why do women live longer than men?
They don't have wives.

A man is having a conversation with God. 'Oh, God,' he asks, 'why did you make women so beautiful?' God replies, 'So you would like them.' 'I see,' the man replies. 'Why did you make women so soft?' Again God replies, 'So you would like them.' The man thinks for a moment and then asks, 'God, why then did you make women so stupid?' God replies, 'So they would like you!'

I take my wife everywhere, but she keeps finding her way back.

Why are married women fatter than single women?
When single women come home they see what's in the refrigerator and go to bed. When married women come home they see what's in bed and go to the refrigerator.

See also **Dumb blondes**; **Husbands and wives**; **Men**.

Work

Wanted. Lad to trace gas leaks with lighted candle. Must be willing to travel.

A man goes to a job interview and is told straightaway he has got the job. He will be paid £12,000 to begin with and £20,000 after six months. 'Excellent,' replies the man. 'I'll come back in six months.'

In what job do you start at the top and work your way down?
Deep sea diver.

'How many people work in this office?'
'About half of them.'

'I've just got a new job as a puppeteer.'
'How did you manage that?'
'I had to pull a few strings.'

'I'm training to be a barber.'
'Is it taking long?'
'No, I'm learning all the short cuts.'

Why did the baker work such long hours?
He kneaded the dough.

Who earns a living by driving customers away?
A taxi-driver.

How do you become a litter collector?
You just pick it up as you go along.

'I'm thinking of becoming a plumber.'
'You might find the work draining.'

What do you call a highly skilled plumber?
A drain surgeon.

A disgruntled employee turns to one of his colleagues and says, 'I feel like punching my boss in the face again.' 'Again?' says the other, surprised. 'Yes,' replies his friend, 'I felt like punching him yesterday.'

Did you hear about the banana inspector who was sacked? He kept slipping up.

Why did the man at the orange juice factory lose his job? He couldn't concentrate.

Why did the elephant give up its job at the factory? It was tired of working for peanuts.

'In a packed programme tonight we will be talking to an out-of-work contortionist who says he can no longer make ends meet.' *(Ronnie Barker)*

See also **Business**; **Punctuality**.

Worms

What is a female worm called?
A worman.

What did the first worm say to the second worm when he came home late?
'Where in earth have you been?'

What happened when two silkworms had a race?
It ended in a tie.

'Doctor, doctor, I keep thinking I'm a woodworm!'
'How boring.'

Y

Yetis See **Abominable snowmen**.

Z

Zebras

What did the idiot call his zebra?
Spot.

What's black and white and goes round and round?
A zebra stuck in a revolving door.

There were ten zebras in the zoo until all but nine escaped.
How many were left?
Nine.

What did the lion say to his cubs when he taught them to hunt?
'Don't go over the road till you see the zebra crossing.'

Zombies

Why did the zombie need to have a rest?
He was dead on his feet.

What do zombies play?
Corpses and robbers.

What jewels do zombies wear?
Tombstones.

What do you call zombie campanologists?
Dead ringers.

Which soup do zombies like best?
Scream of tomato.

Where do zombies play golf?
On the golf corpse.

There was a young zombie named Khan
Who was known for his kindness and charm.
If a stranger or friend
Ever needed a hand
He'd give them a leg or an arm.

What do you get if you cross a zombie with a boy scout?
A monster who scares old ladies across the road.

See also **Abominable snowmen**; **Ghosts**; **Monsters**;
Mummies; **Skeletons**; **Vampires**.

Zoos

Why was the leopard always caught when it tried to
escape from the zoo?
It was always spotted.

Why didn't the zookeeper bother to lock the door to the
lion cage?
He knew no one would steal a lion.

Did you hear about the man who got into trouble for
throwing a £5 note into the monkey enclosure?
The sign said 'Do not feed. £5 fine.'

A police officer stops a motorist and is startled to find he has a dozen penguins on the back seat. 'You shouldn't be driving around with penguins like that,' he tells the man. 'Take them to the zoo.' The man promises he will and the police officer lets him drive off. The next day, however, the police officer stops the same motorist and is annoyed to find the dozen penguins still on his back seat. 'I thought you said you would take these to the zoo, like I told you to!' The man nods. 'I did. And today I'm taking them to the movies.'

See also **Animals**.

He just wanted a decent book to read ...

Not too much to ask, is it? It was in 1935 when Allen Lane, Managing Director of Bodley Head Publishers, stood on a platform at Exeter railway station looking for something good to read on his journey back to London. His choice was limited to popular magazines and poor-quality paperbacks – the same choice faced every day by the vast majority of readers, few of whom could afford hardbacks. Lane's disappointment and subsequent anger at the range of books generally available led him to found a company – and change the world.

'We believed in the existence in this country of a vast reading public for intelligent books at a low price, and staked everything on it'
Sir Allen Lane, 1902–1970, founder of Penguin Books

The quality paperback had arrived – and not just in bookshops. Lane was adamant that his Penguins should appear in chain stores and tobacconists, and should cost no more than a packet of cigarettes.

Reading habits (and cigarette prices) have changed since 1935, but Penguin still believes in publishing the best books for everybody to enjoy. We still believe that good design costs no more than bad design, and we still believe that quality books published passionately and responsibly make the world a better place.

So wherever you see the little bird – whether it's on a piece of prize-winning literary fiction or a celebrity autobiography, political tour de force or historical masterpiece, a serial-killer thriller, reference book, world classic or a piece of pure escapism – you can bet that it represents the very best that the genre has to offer.

Whatever you like to read – trust Penguin.

read more
www.penguin.co.uk